KU-646-833

VANCOUVER
Visions of a City

Vancouver from the North Shore GRAHAM OSBORNE

Concept, Design
and Photo Selection
Karl Spreitz

Editor/Writer
Paul Grescoe

Graphic Design Assistant
and Typographer
Noreen Dennis

Editorial Assistants
Anita Willis
Mary Kruse

Pre-production Assistant
Will Murphy

Cover Photo
Graham Osborne
Vancouver from the North Shore

Fred Herzog,
Photographer

Fred Herzog has been documenting Vancouver since 1957 – "photographing what has been touched by people, used by people, loved by people." Originally a medical photographer (and once honoured as Canada's finest in that demanding field), he was for many years head of the Photo-Cine Division of the Department of Biomedical Communications at the University of British Columbia, where he was also the department's associate director. His work was part of a celebrated three-photographer show, *Extensions,* that the Canada Council and the National Gallery of Canada sent across the country. Many of the photographs in this book are his, including all those bearing dates. And they also bear his trademark of journalism juxtaposed with romanticism and sometimes irony – or what he calls "the humour of humanity."

Published by
Beautiful British Columbia,
a Division of Great Pacific Industries Inc.
John L. Thomson, President;
Tony Owen, Director of Publishing;
Bryan McGill, Editor.

To order copies of this book, call 1-800-663-7611 in Canada and U.S.A. or from Victoria and elsewhere call (604) 384-5456.
Fax: (604) 384-2812

Beautiful British Columbia,
929 Ellery Street,
Victoria, B.C.
V9A 7B4

Printed in Canada by Ronalds Printing, Vancouver, British Columbia on Luna paper produced by Island Paper Mills, Annacis Island, New Westminster, B.C.

Colour separations by WYSIWYG Graphics Inc., Vancouver, B.C.

Binding by Larsens Bookbinding, Langley, B.C.

Canadian Cataloguing in Publication Data

Main entry under title:
Vancouver: Visions of a City
ISBN 0-920431-13-5
1. Vancouver (B.C.). 2. Vancouver (B.C.) -- Pictorial works. I. Beautiful British Columbia Magazine (Firm)
FC3847.37.V35 1993 971.1'33 C93-091387-6
F1089.5.V22V35 1993

Paul Grescoe and Karl Spreitz

City on the Verge

We saw Vancouver for the first time the way so many meet the city: in the thick of winter, when the rest of Canada is rendered white or brown, snowbound and flowerless. We were a young family, fresh off the plane from Toronto via an unscheduled layover in a glacial Edmonton January, and as the taxi took us down a springlike South Granville our hearts leapt at the explosions of green, of growth, detonating all around us. Grand firs and cedars, leafy shrubs and hedges, viridescent lawns that might have been mown only yesterday, and now and then a shock of pink and yellow roses.

Although that was a quarter of a century ago, still seldom a day passes when we don't stare up at the evergreens or flowering cherry trees, look lingeringly down on the sea, or gaze across to the sudden mountains, and record an inward, wondering *Wow!*

The people whose stories are sketched on the following pages share this enthusiasm. They are highly personal symbols of some neighbourhoods, selected suburbs, and unusual aspects of Greater Vancouver — whose occasional criticisms only confirm their love of the place. As does the work of the photographers who portray the city in virtually all of its accents, and of the book's creative director, Karl Spreitz, who shaped their disparate images into a seamless whole. Their striking visions, and the accompanying brief verbal snapshots, can merely hint at what Canada's third-largest metropolis has become since my wife and I moved here with our first child in 1968.

Writers, we had come to a city that was blossoming as artistically as it was blooming naturally. Margaret Atwood had been living not far from where we eventually settled, on the West Side, and the future author of *The Handmaid's Tale* had already written her first book of poetry. In it she explained why she — and we — had come to Vancouver: *we ran west/wanting/a place of absolute/unformed beginning.* And we would agree with her observation, in the same poem, that things here grow from the ground too insistently green to seem spontaneous.

Another author, equally brilliant and about to become a Canadian icon, had a place only a few blocks from us. Margaret Laurence hadn't yet written *The Diviners,* but she had just published *The Fire-Dwellers,* set in Vancouver. She might have been describing our Dunbar neighbourhood when she wrote:

Morning, and the sky is like the light water-color blue from a paintbox. Warm-cool, the air smells of grass and last night's rain. On Bluejay Crescent the laburnum branches bend a little with the yellow wind-swaying burden of blossoms, and the leaves of the big chestnuts are green outspread tree-hands. Kids under school age are out already, whizzing up and down the sidewalks with wagons and tricycles. In the distance, the mountains form the city's walls and boundaries, some of them snow mountains even now, as though this place belonged to two worlds, two simultaneous seasons.

A prairie person, like me, Margaret Laurence never took to Vancouver as home, unlike me. She felt hemmed in by the Pacific and the Coast Mountains; they frightened her. But nature never entraps those who tackle it on its own terms — sailing, swimming, and windsurfing, hiking, climbing, and skiing — or simply appreciate it for its splendour. Of course, not everyone takes to this city: for a few, if the setting isn't all a little overwhelming, then the manmade environment may be altogether underwhelming, and the climate — the definiteness of the rain and the less-defined seasons — dispiriting.

As Harold Kalman, preservation consultant and co-author of *Exploring Vancouver,* once told me, "We've been a little more tasteless than other parts of the country because we seem to take nature for granted, to feel that the mountains can always back us up if we make too big a mistake." But for all the kitschy high-rises and soulless office towers Vancouverites allow, there are many gems, like Richard Henriquez's Sylvia Hotel addition and Arthur Erickson's Robson Square complex — and some of Canada's most intriguing residences, in the timeless post-and-beam, glass-walled, cedar-sided West Coast style that began flourishing in the Fifties and Sixties.

If architecture is an issue of taste, weather is more so. Desert-lovers, season-seekers do not find Vancouver endearing. For the rest of us, the city has one of Canada's most congenial climates — rain notwithstanding. This is written amid the affront of a wintry January, a seldom occurrence, and my shoulders still ache from the unaccustomed shovelling of snow that is never as light and problem-free as the rain. It's true, as ten-year-old Brandon Thompson has written so succinctly: *In Vancouver it really pours,/And people are forced to shut their doors./If you venture out, take your brolly,/But if you have to, take the trolley.* Yes, by God, it can pour in Vancouver, depending on where you live (south Richmond receives about one-third the annual rainfall of North Vancouver's Lynn Creek, which averages 2,700 millimetres). But generally during July and August the city has about half the amount of rain the Prairies get — the least of any major Canadian centre — and there is rarely a night so hot and humid that residents can't sleep. Oh, and we can sit outside all summer without the ritual smacking of mosquitoes that defiles the season everywhere east of this Eden.

Culturally, the city has advanced from the 1930s

THOMAS BRUCKBAUER/IMAGE FINDERS

when British author Graham McInnes wrote a classic critique: "Montreal was exotic and Gallic; Quebec was history; Winnipeg was brash and vigorous; Vancouver had scenery." Vancouverites now spend more money on art, antiques, and decorative ware, and more time book-reading than residents of any other Canadian city. Vancouver has Canada's liveliest independent publishing scene; supports some of the country's finest choirs and early-music organizations; and vies with Toronto as North America's third-busiest film production centre. It was here the continent's first community arts council was born, and the world's first children's festival.

Despite this indulgence in leisure activities, in a genteel climate that encourages them, Vancouverites are not idlers — as the old epithet, "land of the three-hour lunch," would have you believe. Witness the fact that British Columbians, half of whom live in Vancouver, prospered during the recession of the late 1980s and early '90s that rocked the rest of Canada. Adopted son George Woodcock, our most distinguished man of letters and a keen social observer, has said the city is not, "as Eastern Canadians are often prone to assume, a lotus land of easy living. Western prosperity, and expansiveness, are not reared on idleness."

Yet for all its virtues, Vancouver is a city on the verge.

Physically, of course, perched as it is on the western edge of the continental land mass called Canada. Poised on the very rim of the Pacific, on the shores of tomorrow, sharing an ocean with the nations of Asia, where, before century's end, half of all the world's goods and services will originate.

And psychologically too: Vancouver, little more than a century old, lies on the verge of maturity, of what could be an urban greatness fuelled by growth and energy and excellence. The city has a sumptuous sea-and-mountain setting rivalled only by Rio's and Hong Kong's; a vigorous economy based on its role as the nation's busiest port and a pivotal North American gateway for Asians; and a population (1.7 million in 1993) that continues to swell with immigrants, from across the country and around the world, who respond to its soul-expanding natural splendours as well as its income-generating geographical situation. With fifty thousand people moving here each year, this is the fourth-fastest-growing metropolitan area on the continent (after Orlando, Florida, and Sacramento and San Diego, California).

Vancouver is a city, observes the perceptive British travel writer Jan Morris, "that wants to be something else — like a chrysalis approaching metamorphosis. It surely cannot stay as it is forever, eternally young, eternally diffident, defying all odds of urban development....I sense the city worrying its way towards a closer involvement with the world at large."

Diffidence aside, this *is* a young city that has held off some of the more obvious excesses of big metropolises, and now, loping out of its self-centred adolescence, is reaching out to embrace a more involving future in the global community. For the moment — and, with luck and resolve, for the foreseeable future — this will remain a city where we, every Vancouverite and visitor, can greet each day with a *Wow!*

PAUL GRESCOE
Vancouver, 1993

PHOTO OVERLEAF BY AL HARVEY

The First People

When the North West Company fur trader Simon Fraser navigated the river that now bears his name, he had to run wicked rapids and circumvent the fury of Hells Gate in the narrowest reaches of the Fraser Canyon. But nowhere in his eventful journey of 1808 did he meet a more hostile reception than at the wide mouth of the river, in the aboriginal village of Musqueam. On that July day, the villagers fled when his party landed on their shore. Then as he combed through the community, the tide ebbed, leaving his canoe stranded on dry land. "The natives no doubt seeing our difficulty, assumed courage," he wrote in his journal, "and began to make their appearance from every direction, in their coats of mail, howling like so many wolves, and brandishing their war clubs." He and his men escaped upriver.

Nearly two hundred years later, a direct descendant of those warriors figures that Simon Fraser got what he deserved. "The way he treated our people was disrespectful," says Wendy Grant, who served two terms as chief of the Musqueam people and recently became vice-chief for British Columbia of the Assembly of First Nations. The one hundred seventy hectares the Musqueam own along the Fraser's north arm, where it meets the salt-water Strait of Georgia, is Vancouver's oldest neighbourhood — occupied for at least three thousand years. At the time of Fraser's brief stay, there were two thousand aboriginals inhabiting what he called apartments, in a row of houses within a fort "fifteen hundred feet in length and ninety feet in breadth." Today, about eight hundred native people live in a hundred homes on a federal reserve that looks much like the subdivisions it abuts in the city's expensive Southlands district. And the Musqueam are again assuming courage, brandishing verbal clubs to keep what they claim is legitimately theirs — whether land or self-government or fishing rights.

The aboriginal society that Simon Fraser encountered on the coast — and that the Spanish explorers and Captain George Vancouver came upon in the early 1790s — was more highly civilized than any other in the northern half of the continent. With good reason: life was easier here, with a temperate climate and a river, sea, and land rich in food. The Musqueam are the People of the Grass, and deer and elk roamed their grasslands. Edible berries proliferated; today, north of the reserve in the Camosun bog amid Pacific Spirit Park, cloudberry still grows, a remnant of the last Ice Age eleven thousand years ago. Along the Fraser flats, on the Pacific Flyway between South America and Siberia, can be found Canada's densest concentration of wintering waterfowl. But most important of all is the Fraser, which continues to rank among the most abundant salmon rivers in the world.

In 1992 the federal government created a Lower Fraser Fishing Authority that allocated 395,000 sockeye salmon and lesser numbers of other varieties to aboriginal groups, who can sell a percentage on the open market. Non-native commercial and sport fishermen, severely limited in their catches, have protested. The Musqueam people, who launched a Supreme Court lawsuit that enshrined their aboriginal fishing rights, are holding firm. As a girl, Wendy Grant went salmon-fishing with her father, and even now twenty percent of her people make their living from the ancient waterways. "The

Wendy Grant, as a vice-chief of the Assembly of First Nations today, and as a child on the reserve in 1953, standing on the right.

fishing issue represents, more than anything else, what our place in society really is," she says. "It goes to the very heart of who we are. Historically, fish were revered — they were not just something you ate."

At forty-five, a mother of four, Wendy Grant has poignant memories of a way of life on the Musqueam that has long since gone, a time when homes had no electricity or running water. "I cry for my kids that they don't have the freedom, and the ability to connect with who they are as aboriginal people. You could be gone all day here, playing in the woods and on the mudflats along the river, and your Mom didn't worry about you. Each house was your house. And the elders would talk about what you should be doing."

Her uncle and then her grandfather were Musqueam chiefs. She was the first of ten children born to an aboriginal father, Willard Sparrow, and his Scottish-Norwegian wife, Helen, the first white woman to live on the reserve. Wendy grew up working alongside her father on the fishboats and, when he was elected chief, became band secretary. It was a safe world compared with the one she faced in predominantly white schools in the middle-class neighbourhoods near the reserve. Except for two sympathetic teachers, she says, "I have no good memories of going to school. It wasn't hate I felt; it was like you didn't exist." She remembers as a ten-year-old lying in her bed at night and dreaming of telling her schoolmates: "One day soon you're going to have to look at me and we're going to settle our claim and you'll have to go back to Europe. Judy Nightingale and Margaret White can stay because they're nice to me." She can still feel the fear of walking to school — "that's what gives me the drive to succeed, so no other children on the reserve have to feel that."

She took native studies during Grade Twelve at the Institute of Adult Studies in Victoria and then briefly at the University of Waterloo. At nineteen she married a boy she'd grown up with on the reserve. Howard Grant, of mixed Chinese and aboriginal parents, was studying physical education at university. While he wound up with the Department of Indian Affairs (and more recently became local band manager), his wife raised their children, worked on federal grant projects on the reserve, and founded a weaving group. Her great-great-great-grandmother, Spakiya, had been the last of the traditional

GRAHAM OSBORNE

weavers who created works of art from mountain-goat wool, dog hair and even duck down. Some of the blankets were for everyday use, but the chiefs flaunted special ones as signs of wealth at intertribal potlatch ceremonies. Wendy Grant formed a group of women, the Musqueam Weavers, who revived the art on two-bar stationary looms, travelling across the continent to compare techniques and study examples of their ancestors' blankets in museums. "The ancestral knowledge was so strong," she recalls, "these women picked it up in six months."

It wasn't until she reached thirty, when her middle son was born with a heart problem, that Wendy Grant realized she had to shed the anger in her own heart and connect with white people. "Sitting in intensive care after he had open-heart surgery, watching all these loving, compassionate people look after my child, I started recognizing the importance of relating to the non-aboriginal community. I guess I had deadened myself for so long."

Eight years later, she was ripe for the job when her fellow weavers urged her to run for Musqueam chief. By the end of her second term, as this elegantly composed woman with the ebony hair and walnut eyes spoke out eloquently on self-government and Canadian constitutional issues, her influence had grown — enough to prompt a local business magazine to name her one of B.C.'s "power elite." She likens the job of chief to being mayor, premier, prime minister, and family counsellor all in one. Among the city's largest landowners,

Musqueam leases most of its prime land — for two golf courses and two housing developments — but only in recent years has it negotiated agreements that offer the band a reasonable return. This was one of the first three Canadian reserves to start levying property taxes on subdivisions located on its leased land, generating more than $800,000 a year. The band also acquired 3.2 hectares of Crown land on the Fraser to launch Celtic Shipyards, where Musqueam apprentices learn their trade alongside qualified journeymen, building fireboats for the City of Vancouver and small people-powered submersibles for University of British Columbia engineering students.

Throughout Greater Vancouver, the Musqueam and other Coast Salish peoples control some of the finest foreshore property. Two decades ago, the Squamish Band on the North Shore began making joint-venture deals for hotel and retail development. The two hundred members of the Burrard Band of North Vancouver have recently leased two hectares of reserve land along the Burrard Inlet to a bank and a developer, both Asian-based, to build a hundred luxury condominiums in a profit-sharing project that could return the band up to $10 million.

Two centuries ago, as Wendy Grant well knows, the Coast Salish had all the land and the water to themselves. Now there are few places in Vancouver that can conjure up a vision of what once was. So we treasure the four hundred hectares of Stanley Park, a verdant peninsula of lawns and forests, fringed by the sea and soothingly situated on the verge of the downtown. The largest natural park of any Canadian city, it is both lordly wildwood and English country garden — what might result if Robinson Crusoe moved in with Mary Poppins. As Bruce Hutchison wrote in *The Unknown Country*, "it was one of the few sensible things done in our youth, the preservation of this sweep of timber in the centre of a large city, with its beaches, rocks and cliffs, undefiled." The Vancouver Public Aquarium is there, one of the continent's finest, a reminder of the prolific life in surrounding Burrard Inlet, part of the nation's busiest port.

Salish people, living at what is now Lumberman's Arch in Stanley Park, once rowed out into this inlet to meet the yawl and the launch of an English captain named Vancouver. Today, three thousand ships of ninety nations dock here annually, goliaths up to ninety-four-thousand deadweight tonnes escorted into harbour by pushy little tugboats. The freighters load grain and sulphur and other raw materials, more than sixty-six-million tonnes a year. They share the harbour with sailboats, motor launches, sea planes, and the SeaBuses ferrying commuters downtown from the North Shore forty-two-thousand times each year.

Wendy Grant observes all the changes — the land blanketed with houses and high-rises, the waterways thick with big ships and logging booms — and asks the question: "In order to be perceived as successful in the non-aboriginal world, what do you have to give up?" As provincial vice-chief of the Assembly of First Nations, she believes the ways of her people have something to offer the larger society. "I think it's going to be easier," she says simply and with not a trace of arrogance, "once we help non-Indian people learn who they are and how they relate to us."

DAVE WATTERS/IMAGE FINDERS

The sanctuaries of our immense parks continue to soothe the city's soul

DUNCAN McDOUGALL/DIARAMA

AL HARVEY

The 400 hectares of Stanley Park, *above*, form a grand green patch on the downtown; Pacific Spirit Park, *left*, is a remnant of all the land the Musqueam people once knew intimately.

DAVE WATTERS/IMAGE FINDERS

The concrete columns of the Museum of Anthropology – a shrine to native art – echo a totem pole overlooking the sea, where the salt water meets the Fraser River that continues to feed local aboriginal people.

FRED HERZOG

The salmon-rich Fraser River has nurtured the First Nations people for centuries

RICK BLACKLAWS

PETER BENNETT

THOMAS KITCHIN

PETER BENNETT

This is the nation's busiest port, where the shipping container was invented decades ago

PETER BENNETT

PETER TIMMERMANS

Sharing the port with pleasure vessels, three thousand ships of ninety nations meet transcontinental trains here as they load grain, coal, and lumber.

1954

CPR Pier

FRED HERZOG

THOMAS KITCHIN

Heart and Soul

Across the street, in MacLean Park, a trio of elderly Chinese women perform their tai chi exercises with slow, swanlike movements. Two middle-aged native men perch on a park bench, speaking from time to time as they wallow in the winter sun. A couple of blocks away, morning shoppers are picking up salt cod and home-baked cornbread from Mrs. Gomes' Portuguese grocery, and salami and *panettone* from Benny's Italian Market, which has stood on the same corner since 1915. And in a four-year-old mock-Victorian house overlooking the park, Wendy Newman watches as her toddling daughter, Rosa, ritualistically kisses her honorary godmother goodbye through the glass of the patio door.

Rosa and her septuagenarian godmother, Poh Poh, are Chinese. Wendy Newman, of Jewish- and English-Canadian stock, was the first single woman in Canada allowed to adopt an infant from mainland China. In 1992, at the age of forty-four, the arts consultant brought Rosa from an orphanage on the Yangtze River in Central China to her inner-city home in Strathcona on the yeasty Downtown East Side.

Mother and daughter met Poh Poh in MacLean Park one day, after discreetly letting the Chinese-godmother grapevine know that Rosa needed someone of her own culture to care for her five times a week. Poh Poh, with parchment skin and gold teeth flashing through her beatific smile, speaks no English; she is teaching Rosa Cantonese — and much more than a second language.

Wendy Newman, as a child in 1952, and as the first single Canadian woman to adopt a child from China – charming Rosa.

"This is absolutely the best neighbourhood in which to raise a child from China, to fulfill that dream of raising a child in two cultures," Wendy Newman says. Bordering on North America's second-largest Chinatown and Vancouver's birthplace — Gastown — Strathcona was the first real neighbourhood to develop after the city's founding in 1886 at the terminus of the nation-building Canadian Pacific Railway.

The promise of Burrard Inlet had begun attracting people a quarter of a century earlier. A sea captain named Edward Stamp set up his sawmill at the waterfront end of what is now the Downtown East Side's Dunlevy Street. Logging camps lured the entrepreneurial John Deighton, who came by canoe from the colony's (and Western Canada's) first incorporated city, nearby New Westminster. Gassy Jack Deighton set up a flourishing saloon and lent his nickname to the new townsite of Granville — more familiarly known as Gastown, for the loquacious saloon-keeper. Two months after its rebirth as the City of Vancouver, the thousand inhabitants watched most of their four blocks of wooden buildings burn down, but by the end of 1886 eight thousand people were supporting fifty-one stores, twenty-three hotels, nine saloons, and one church (oh, and a roller-skating rink).

The Anglo-Saxon gentry moved a little east to set up residence in a neighbourhood named for the first Baron Strathcona and Mount Royal, the railroad financier Donald Smith, who drove the CPR's last ceremonial spike. By the turn of the century Strathcona's original settlers had given way to a stew of immigrant families: Italian, Russian, Scandinavian, Yugoslav, and Japanese, who moved into the outsized frame dwellings, turning many of them into rooming houses for miners, fishermen, and loggers. European Jews, Ukrainians, and more Russians followed, escaping Old Country pogroms and poverty; Chinese, seeking the fabled Gold Mountain; and blacks, fleeing the Depression-flattened Prairies. After 1947, as prospering immigrants moved out of Strathcona, Canada repealed the restrictive Chinese Immigration Act and a fresh surge of families poured into the working-class neighbourhood from China, refuelling Chinatown.

Today both Strathcona and Gastown are being transformed by artists, professionals and other non-immigrant residents choosing to live within the inner city. Although Gastown warehouse lofts are being remodelled for apartments, much of the area remains a tarted-up yet appealing tourist destination — a cornucopia of restaurants and intriguing curio shops, cobblestoned streets, a clock powered by steam, and a statue of Gassy Jack in Maple Tree Square, the cultural centre of the old town.

Strathcona, at the heart of the modern city, remains the conservator of much of its soul. Not only because of the multiplicity of its churches: Russian Orthodox, Chinese Mennonite, Vietnamese Christian, and Buddhist, along with the elegant-spired St. Francis Xavier Catholic Church on East Pender, which once was Swedish Evangelical Lutheran, and (across from the police station), the octagonal-roofed St. James Anglican, a concrete Gothic Revival church that many Vancouverites consider the city's most handsome building.

No, what also makes Strathcona special is its sense of community. Despite having the second-lowest median incomes in Canada, the people of the neighbourhood have a history of fiercely protecting and preserving their turf. In the late 1960s, their protests stopped a freeway from scarring the community, and the Strathcona Property Owners and Tenants Association forced city hall to rehabilitate rather than bulldoze the old housing stock — half of which was built before 1946.

More recently, the Strathcona Citizens Planning Committee formed spontaneously to combat the pressures of crime spilling over from nearby Hastings Street and speculators razing heritage houses for high-rises. The committee was crucial in creating the city's Strathcona Plan, which insists that locals have a voice in the kinds of development the neighbourhood will absorb. This led to one of Vancouver's first community-policing experiments, where two officers are assigned full-time to the area, working out of Strathcona Community Centre. Their role is to prevent crime, rather than merely respond to it. Not long ago, they convinced an apartment landlord to squeeze out his drug-dealer and prostitute tenants, renovate the building, and rent to ordinary folk. The police also work with a citizens' midnight patrol group, which decided on direct action to harass the dealers and hookers off residential streets and parks.

No matter how incongruous a setting others might consider Strathcona, Wendy Newman would live nowhere else now. The daughter of socially active leftists, she grew up in more genteel circumstances: what's been described as the first modern house in Greater Vancouver, a sprawling Bauhaus-inspired place with a special child's-scale wing in safe, suburban Burnaby. Dancing and acting, she had a culturally rich childhood (a grandfather, Stanley Bligh, was *The Vancouver Sun's* dance and music critic for decades). Her Jewish father was in the family furniture business and her English mother became a high-school art teacher. After university, Wendy wound up second-in-command at the Vancouver East Cultural Centre and later executive director of the legendary Cultch, which has become the city's most eclectic performing space.

Freelancing as an arts consultant, she's living in Strathcona for the second time, in a two-storey, bay-windowed house she bought in 1988 and now shares with Rosa. She explains her daughter's name: "Rosa, because of her little rosebud mouth, and because I love gardens — and nurturing a child is like gardening." Wendy has a plot in the Strathcona Community Garden, a 1.5 hectare oasis of a hundred organic plots, an orchard and natural habitat tended by about two hundred locals, many of them retired Chinese like Rosa's Poh Poh.

"There may be a bamboo curtain between communities in Strathcona," Wendy Newman says, "but with Rosa and Poh Poh I may be one of the few who are getting through it."

PETER TIMMERMANS

KEN STRAITON/IMAGE FINDERS

FRED HERZOG

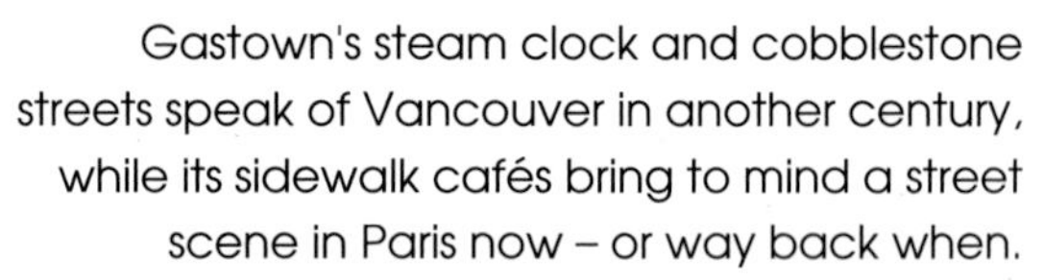
Gastown's steam clock and cobblestone streets speak of Vancouver in another century, while its sidewalk cafés bring to mind a street scene in Paris now – or way back when.

THOMAS BRUCKBAUER/IMAGE FINDERS

Gastown, no longer an inner-city ghetto, surprises with its agreeable streetscape

FRED HERZOG

AL HARVEY

Strathcona's sense of community makes this neighbourhood the special place it is

FRED HERZOG

FRED HERZOG

PETER TIMMERMANS

Hastings Street

1955

FRED HERZOG

On the verge of the dense, darkly exciting Downtown Eastside, old Strathcona remains what it began as: a real neighbourhood, chock-full of churches, children, and their house-proud parents.

FRED HERZOG

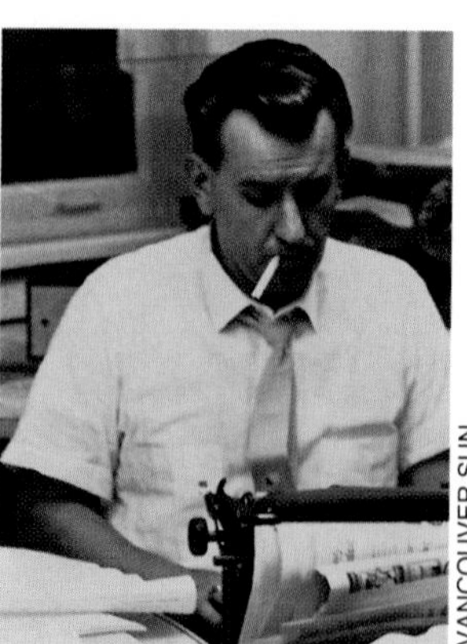
VANCOUVER SUN

The sea is breathing in small, half-hearted waves and Frisbees hiss through the air like plates at a Greek wedding. Hopping stiffly, crows make their meagre living as night-time janitors. It is a gentle time here, in the closing sun, in a place where the sea and land have struck up an irreversible alliance, one bridge away from the downtown skirmish zones.

Some great cities bestow on their suburbs little but the means to an inferiority complex, a demeaning sense of smallness accentuated by nearby bigness. But Vancouver suburbs breathe their own air and march to the beat of a different heart.

Some suburbs might dispute their priorities on the Genesis job list. West Vancouver merely claims to have been designed by God on His day off....

His Kind Of Town

That is the unmistakable gruff/gentle voice of Denny Boyd, the *Vancouver Sun* columnist who has been chronicling Greater Vancouver for more than a decade and a half — while carrying on a love-hate relationship with West Vancouver, where he lives alone in a ninth-floor waterfront penthouse. From his balcony, he has a multimillionaire's prospect of city and seascape, of the sailboats and freighters and cruise ships gliding beneath the Lions Gate Bridge, past sky-poking office towers and the grand green patch of Stanley Park.

This is still heady stuff for the boy from Anyox, a copper town on the B.C. coast that has long since given up the ghost. The boy grew up to be a squat plug of a man, with an Irishman's gift for the word and a face like a slightly dissolute leprechaun's, roseate from all the publicly proclaimed drinking days that are well behind him. "Here I am," he says, "a kid from an ugly company town, a place with an orange slough — you couldn't call it a river — and I'm living in the richest community in Canada." West Vancouverites routinely enjoy the highest average annual income in Canada ($48,500, at last count).

Denny Boyd has lived in other suburbs, including North Vancouver, which shares the North Shore and the abrupt Coast Mountains backdrop with its wealthier cousin — but little else. "If West Van is driving a $275,000 cherry-red Rolls-Royce," he says, "then North Van is taking a bus." The distinctions between them begin at the foot of the mountains, on the waterfront, where West Vancouver is thirty kilometres of marinas and yacht clubs, high-rise residences and private homes, forty percent of it parkland, including a seawall walk. North Vancouver's foreshore is a belt of gritty wharves, grain elevators, shipyards, rail terminals, and an enormous yellow mound of sulphur that stains the view.

From the start, the 1860s, North Van was anchored by a firm industrial base. Known as Moodyville, it had a large shoreline sawmill owned by Sewell Moody that shipped knot-free timber around the world, and as the original non-native community on Burrard Inlet, had the first school, library, and electric lights north of San Francisco. During the same decade, West Vancouver's first white settler was Navvy Jack Thomas, who sold gravel and ran a ferry. When fitful logging operations faded after the turn of the century, the community became a tent-and-cottage hamlet, the only real industry a fish cannery.

Denny Boyd, as sports reporter in 1957, and as columnist and Greater Vancouver chronicler today.

With a population of 39,000, West Vancouver still has virtually no manufacturing. Ever genteel, it introduced B.C.'s first poop-and-scoop law, and for years had a mayor who dictated the colour of shopkeepers' awnings. Until recently, North Vancouver (pop. 113,600) has made do with a plain-Jane commercial centre; now the elegantly designed Lonsdale Quay market is encouraging a rebirth of the harbour district. In contrast, its North Shore neighbour has the village-like Dundarave shopping area and the freshly refurbished Park Royal, Western Canada's first shopping centre. While North Van's homes are more conventional and much lower-priced, West Van's set a Canadian standard for architecture after the Second World War with their long, low, glass-and-wood responsiveness to the landscape. That sympathy with site began even earlier, in the 1930s, when the Guinness brewing family of Britain saved West Van from bankruptcy by buying 1,700 hectares of mountainside for $75,000 and carving out the British Pacific Properties — today, just The Properties — with sensitive landscaping. They also built one of the continent's best golf courses, Capilano Golf and Country Club, and the graceful span of Lions Gate Bridge to bring people from Vancouver to live in the upscale subdivision. (The Second Narrows Bridge, way off to the east, went up two decades later, but not before twenty-three men died when it collapsed during construction.)

Lions Gate, which is showing its age, is named for the pair of leonine peaks that loom 1,770 metres over the city. North Vancouver's mountain wilderness always seems more at hand than its cousin's, with deer and black bear routinely dropping into backyards. Canadian composer Michael Conway-Baker's house and recording studio back onto the Seymour River in the Blueridge residential area; not long ago, hearing a thump outside, he saw a cougar prowling his deck. North Van's Grouse and Seymour mountains have the serious local ski slopes (and a dizzying, 1.6-kilometre-long aerial tram-ride up Grouse to a decent restaurant at the 1,130-metre level). Its richer rival's Hollyburn and Cypress Bowl are more for family and cross-country skiing. West Van does, however, offer the seventy-five seaside hectares of Lighthouse Park, set amid five-century-old Douglas firs rising sixty metres above the nature trails. And its farthest western reaches terminate in the tiny, poster-pretty port of Horseshoe Bay, where ferries embark for Nanaimo, the Sechelt Peninsula, and the rapidly gentrifying refuge of nearby Bowen Island, fast becoming a bedroom suburb for commuters.

GRAHAM OSBORNE

West Vancouver is Denny Boyd's home of choice, despite its previous reputation for being frightfully well-bred, discreetly racist, and so eccentrically Anglophile that *Sun* cartoonist Len Norris labelled it "Tiddlycove." Now a fifth of its seniors receive some form of social assistance, and even in the exclusive Properties, more than a quarter of the homeowners are Asian and Middle Eastern — the Ismaili Muslims' fabulously wealthy Aga Khan has maintained a residence in the subdivision (heck, Boyd himself once rented a house there with a pool bordering on the golf course).

On a Saturday morning, the columnist might leave his seaside penthouse to stroll over to Marine Drive, picking up steamy bread, freshly ground coffee, and a book from the library on which he served as a board member, and which still has the highest per-capita lending rate in Canada. Or thinking about a column, he'll walk the seawall the half-hour from Ambleside Park to his favourite place, the Dundarave Pier, where he'll watch the scoters and cormorants creasing the water, and Asian newcomers hauling up a perch or small tommycod to take home for dinner. With a visitor in tow, he points out one of the nicest undiscovered beaches in Vancouver, a sandy strand beside the pier. "And there's Vancouver Island," he says, staring out at the Strait of Georgia, "and beyond that is Japan, I guess." Then he stops and confesses: "There's still a little feeling in me of 'By God, I did get to live here!'"

DALE SANDERS

The Capilano River tumbles down from the North Shore Mountains into a harbour plied by the world's freighters and by pleasure boats passing beneath the Second Narrows Bridge.

AL HARVEY

The Coast Mountains create an abrupt backdrop for the two cities

DUNCAN MCDOUGALL/DIARAMA

AL HARVEY

Genteel and wild, the North Shore nestles amid the mountains

PETER TIMMERMANS

Sail Past

1960

FRED HERZOG

DOUG NEALY/IMAGE FINDERS

PETER TIMMERMANS

PHILIP/KAREN SMITH

West Vancouverites ski on the North Shore slopes, golf on the Properties' Capilano course, shop in village-like Dundarave, and live in cliff-hugging houses that have set Canadian architectural standards.

"A place where sea and land have an irreversible alliance"

AL HARVEY

GORDON J. FISHER/IMAGE FINDERS

KOOS DYKSTRA/IMAGE FINDERS

The West Vancouver shoreline offers smelt fishing, Lighthouse Park, and the ferries of Horseshoe Bay, *below*; North Vancouver has St. Paul's Catholic Church overlooking the Burrard Yacht Club and the workaday wharves that load freighters with lumber and sulphur.

PHILIP/KAREN SMITH

GUNTER MARX

Making It

Joe Segal, as a hopeful young businessman in Vancouver, 1947, and as university chancellor today.

Joe Segal had a life-shaking decision to make. It was June 1978 and the chairman of Zellers Limited, a moderate-sized chain of Canadian discount department stores, had to weigh whether to launch a surprising takeover bid for the Hudson's Bay Company, a $5-billion-a-year merchandising conglomerate on its way to becoming Canada's major retailing presence. He had already arranged the complex $450-million financing for a fifty-one-percent share of the nation's original business empire. But what gave him pause was the reality that, if he were successful, he would have to leave the city he loved, Vancouver.

While overseeing the turnaround of Zellers, Segal had spent the past three years commuting to Montreal with his wife, Rosalie. Their home here was one of the West Coast's most magnificent mansions, *Rio Vista*, a Spanish Colonial Revival with a palatial conservatory growing California-large fruit and enclosing a swimming pool of Pompeiian splendour.

Now Rosalie was asking him why he wanted to bother wresting control of Hudson's Bay, which would take them away from home again. "Do you need the money?" she asked rhetorically. "No," he allowed. "But it's a great opportunity." "Well, do what you want," his wife said. "But I'm telling you now, I'm not going to commute with you."

Fifteen years later, Joe Segal muses over his fateful decision: "I could have taken over The Bay, but I wouldn't leave Vancouver — and that's the literal truth."

Today the financier and philanthropist, nearing his seventies, controls a melange of companies that make everything from materials-handling equipment to baby furniture, from steel shelving to clothing — Mr. Jax is a major women's-wear manufacturer expanding rapidly in the U.S. He sits surrounded by fine Inuit art in his office at the very axis of Vancouver's downtown: the black-sheathed IBM Tower at Granville and Georgia, just a few blocks from where it all began for him in this city more than forty years before.

The town centre has endured the strains and dislocations common to all of Canada's urban areas, but, with the dizzying growth of the Lower Mainland, continues to redefine — indeed, reinvent — itself. The tower housing Segal's Kingsland Capital Corporation rises atop the Pacific Centre, an underground labyrinth of shopping malls, department stores, and a hotel. In the early 1970s this project shifted the centre of gravity from his, and the city's, old stomping ground of Hastings Street. He has since committed himself to help revive the street through a development that someday may be seen as the beginning of Hastings' renaissance: the creation of a downtown campus for Simon Fraser University, of which he recently became chancellor.

Every great Western city has an institution of higher learning within its core, easily accessible to its citizens — whereas SFU is based way out east in Burnaby and the University of British Columbia in Vancouver's westernmost reaches on the Point Grey waterfront. And Joe Segal believes that any university with a survival instinct must have the support of the business community. What better way to make SFU relevant than by locating an active satellite campus downtown, where business people can learn Mandarin and Cantonese in the evening and earn a Master's of Business Administration on weekends?

Segal and his wife not only made substantial financial contributions to the university's campaign for an inner-city campus but, as an SFU governor and skilled deal-maker, he also worked out the terms for an unconventional win-win lease to house it. He did that on a napkin over lunch with university vice-president Jack Blaney in the Four Seasons Hotel's swank Chartwell restaurant. In 1989 Simon Fraser opened what has become a growing branch plant in Harbour Centre, the former Sears Tower at Seymour and Hastings.

Six blocks away lies Maple Leaf Square in Gastown, around which Vancouver grew from an embryonic railway terminus at its 1886 incorporation to a toddling town of ten thousand by decade's end. One of its most influential shapers was David Oppenheimer, who, with his brother Isaac, had run stores during the gold rush in B.C.'s

GRAHAM OSBORNE

Cariboo before becoming one of Vancouver's earliest local real-estate investors. As the city's second mayor and arguably its best, German-born David Oppenheimer set the tone for philanthropy in Vancouver's Jewish community, a tradition that business people like Joe Segal continue a century later. Oppenheimer served without pay, financed all the administrative expenses of his position, and contributed some of his own land for schools and parks. During his tenure, the city acquired Stanley Park, set up the YMCA and a civic orphanage, and established the water supply and a street railway.

The Oppenheimer brothers were sharp gamblers at cards as well as real estate. The story goes that a sleepy poker player had awoken from an instant nap to find he held four queens in his hand. Who dealt this round? he asked. David. Who cut the deck? Ike. I pass, he said.

Little more than a decade later, gambling of a more institutional nature began with the opening of the Vancouver Stock Exchange in 1907. Among the first to buy a seat was Constantin Gustav Alvo von Alvensleben, born of German nobility, who became the first of the high-flying stock promoters with fly-by-night reputations that colour the Exchange to this day. The Count's funnelling of European money to Canada made him as much as $25 million before the 1913 depression did him in and the Custodian of Enemy Aliens seized all his property during the First World War.

During the Second World War another gambler, a fledgling named Joe Segal, lost everything he'd saved as a pick-and-shovel labourer helping build the Alaska Highway. After dropping the $3,000 in a poker game on his first night holidaying in Calgary, he signed up for the infantry. In 1946, after two years with the Calgary Highlanders, he came to Vancouver to visit his mother. He was smitten — by a girl named Rosalie and by the city. "Let's face it," he says, "this is not a very difficult city to fall in love with."

It was on West Hastings where, after dabbling in the war-surplus trade and real estate, Joe Segal set up the first of a chain of Fields clothing stores. It sat between the Army & Navy bargain store, which is still there, and the flagship Woodward's department store, which as of 1993 is not. Fields neighboured on Pioneer Park, now known as Pigeon Park for the birds that vie with the down-and-outers who have staked the war memorial as their turf. "Hastings was alive," he says. Today the street is only beginning to revive, helped along by the Heimlich manoeuvres of SFU's further expansion at Harbour Centre and a local developer's hopeful plans for the old Woodward's building.

Segal strides the downtown with a commingling of regret for what's gone and pleasure in what has replaced it or is promised. He looks forward to two $100-million developments scheduled to open by 1995 along Georgia Street on the eastern verges of the core: a multi-purpose arena for the National Hockey League's Vancouver Canucks (and perhaps for a National Basketball Association franchise), and a monumental library complex in the shape of a spiralling Colosseum. His office, more centrally located on Georgia at Granville, is at a pivotal corner in Vancouver's development. Eaton's moved there from Hastings to face off against its merchandising rival, The Bay, and the Pacific Centre development moved people underground, robbing the crossroads of some of its vigour — a process hastened by the closing of Granville Mall to cars. What Granville has lost, nearby Robson has gained in energy as a retailing street that attracts a tumult of teenagers on summer evenings and a multitude of Asian visitors year-round. And Robson Square, with its covered skating rink and sleek low-rise Law Courts structure spreading over two blocks, has become the nearest thing to a city centre.

Across the street, with its original entrance fronting on Georgia Street, hulks the eight-decade-old Court House, a handsome sandstone-and-granite pile that's now the Vancouver Art Gallery. Along with the château-like Hotel Vancouver next door, it is among the city's handsomest heritage buildings. Another exquisite pair, which share a late-1920s vintage, are the Orpheum Theatre along Granville (the rococo home of the Vancouver Symphony), and the tall brick Marine Building at Burrard and Hastings, heavily ornamented with 1920s art deco relief and storytelling terracotta panels.

Throughout the expansive 1980s, the city centre began widening eastward. One influence was the sixty-thousand-seat B.C. Place, which rose on the northern

A city's institutions: the trading floor of the Vancouver Stock Exchange; city hall as seen from the turn-of-the-century dome of Carnegie Centre; and the modernistic dome of Canada Place in the distance.

KOOS DYKSTRA/IMAGE FINDERS

AL HARVEY

ROGER BROOKS

shore of False Creek. The playing field of the Canadian Football League's B.C. Lions (and someday, it's hoped, of a professional baseball team), this was Canada's first covered stadium and the world's largest air-supported domed amphitheatre. Then, in the wake of Expo 86, one of the century's more successful world's fairs, the silver sphere of the Expo Preview Centre became Science World, with the largest-ever domed movie screen. And the former Canadian Pavilion on the downtown waterfront became Canada Place, housing a hotel, office tower, and the Vancouver Trade and Convention Centre. Set beneath a roofline of five billowing white sails, the complex has a superstructure as elegant as those of the seagoing liners tying up at its cruise-ship terminal.

In summer, Joe Segal enjoys walking down to Canada Place to peer up at the big ships and people-watch. "Downtown isn't a total bustle-and-build kind of environment," he says. "It's a little slower-paced. You can always go to the beach and to Stanley Park." Few urban cores have nature on their very doorstep the way Vancouver does, the sandy shore and the parkland so easily accessible to tens of thousands dwelling downtown in the West End. In the 1960s the city skyscape began to mirror the mountain backdrop as residential high-rises soared in the square mile of the West End. This has become one of Canada's most thickly populated areas — and, with penthouses that sell for $3 million to $5 million, perhaps the country's priciest concentration of condominiums.

"Today," Joe Segal observes, speaking of office buildings he once bought for a pittance, "you can't buy a shack for less than $1 million." The lofty prices merely reflect the confidence the city continues to engender in local and international investors. "I believe that, in Canadian terms, Vancouver has the brightest future," he says. "And as long as people are employed, this will be the greatest place to live in the world." Somehow you know he means it, this man who wouldn't leave here even to buy the Hudson's Bay Company.

Business is conducted amid white-capped peaks and a sailboat-studded harbour

PETER TIMMERMANS

From the perspective of Stanley Park, the downtown rears up on the south shore of Burrard Inlet, *below*. A sampling of stunning architecture, new and old: the Vancouver Bank of Commerce, *top left*, the Toronto Dominion Tower on West Georgia, *middle left*, and Park Place on Burrard, *bottom left*.

STEVEN SHORT/IMAGE FINDERS

MARIN PETKOV/IMAGE FINDERS

GORDON J. FISHER/IMAGE FINDERS

Few urban cores have nature poised so dramatically on their doorsteps as Vancouver does

AL HARVEY

With the city's dizzying growth, downtown continues to redefine – and reinvent – itself

Granville Street

1966

FRED HERZOG

GRAHAM OSBORNE

MARIN PETKOV/IMAGE FINDERS

Style meets substance in the city centre: dwarfed by office towers, the neoclassical Vancouver Art Gallery, *opposite page*, Cathedral Place and the Hong Kong Bank building, post-modern neighbours, *left*; and lushly landscaped Robson Square and Arthur Erickson's provincial Law Courts complex.

AL HARVEY

MARIN PETKOV/IMAGE FINDERS

MICHAEL MONG

Sounds of the city: a helicopter harrumphing over the downtown; workers slapping on plaster in a construction ballet; and football fans erupting in domed B.C. Place Stadium.

AL HARVEY

Robson Street

1965

FRED HERZOG

Rising to the occasion, Canada's third-largest city continues to achieve new heights in work and play

GUNTER MARX

Commercial Hotel

1966

FRED HERZOG

An anthill of commercial activity, the inner city can also be a lonely place to live

MICHAEL MONG

While a solitary figures gazes from an inner-city hotel, daredevils in hard hats create a new high-rise; a workman polishes the art-deco façade of the 1930 Marine Building; and the Vancouver Symphony performs on Granville Island.

GRANT V. FAINT

AL HARVEY

Cornelia Oberlander in 1953, and the landscape architect in her own beloved garden today.

West Side Story

Consider the cold statistics. In a city that collectively thumbed its nose at the recent recession, house prices remained the highest in Canada, and they were at their loftiest on Vancouver's West Side. The city has more land zoned for single-family housing than any major centre on the continent — seventy per cent — and the West Side is where such zoning flourishes. And the nation's wealthiest young singles, men and women, live on this side of town. Yet what makes this agglomeration of neighbourhoods so eminently livable cannot be measured alone by the cost and kind of housing, the level of income — or by the area's strategic situation between the airport and downtown. The West Side is also sought after for less mercenary, more natural attributes: the 'round-every-corner parks, the necklace of exquisite beaches, and the verdant streetscapes that define Vancouver as a city of trees.

If any one person can symbolize this essential character of the region — bounded by the University of British Columbia on the west and Ontario Street on the east, by the Fraser River on the south and Burrard Inlet on the north — it is Cornelia Oberlander. Canada's pre-eminent landscape architect, she came here in her late twenties from the American Eastern Seaboard four decades ago, and lives on UBC's lush Endowment Lands with her husband, the architect and educator Peter Oberlander. In 1970, on a supposedly unbuildable lot, they subtly wedged a long, two-storey, modernist house on concrete pillars above a ravine that is part of Pacific Spirit Park. The views are over the inlet towards the North Shore Mountains — whose majesty took her ten years of skiing and hiking to get used to.

She fell faster, harder, for the park in her backyard that cuts a 750-hectare swath between Vancouver's westernmost residential district and the campus. "When we become overbuilt," she says, "this will be one of the most important lungs of the city." Pacific Spirit epitomizes the greenery and natural grace of the West Side, a feral forest in which to escape the urban jungle. Well-marked trails wend through uplifting fir and cedar that were last fully logged in 1905.

Come spring, she visits the VanDusen Botanical Gardens — twenty-two serene hectares of lawns, ponds, native and exotic plants, and teaching and propagation facilities — to walk through what may be the finest collection of rhododendrons in the country. Any mild day, she might find herself in Queen Elizabeth Park, amid the waterfalls and sunken gardens hewn out of quarries. Here, on Little Mountain, the City of Vancouver's highest point, she re-experiences the plaza with the walk-through Henry Moore sculpture and the domed Bloedel Conservatory luxuriant with tropical plants.

Cornelia Oberlander has landscaped major projects for two of Canada's most internationally renowned architects: Moshe Safdie's National Gallery of Canada in Ottawa and his Colosseumlike Vancouver Public Library, scheduled for completion in 1995; and Arthur Erickson's Canadian Embassy in Washington and his oasislike Robson Square complex in the heart of his hometown, Vancouver. Among her favourite commissions is the work she did on the West Side for Erickson's monumental Museum of Anthropology at UBC, planted with grasses and other vegetation used by local native people, whose art and craft is showcased within.

The museum rises on a cliff overlooking the beaches that stretch along the West Side's northern and western perimeters. Wreck Beach, a rocky, isolated strand for nudists (which TV's *Lives of the Rich and Famous* declared one of the world's top ten beaches). The largest, the sandy, family-oriented Spanish Banks. And perhaps the best all-round, Kitsilano Beach, for swimming and windsurfing, basketball and volleyball. Cornelia Oberlander's preference is expansive Jericho Beach Park, where seniors from a nearby housing complex can saunter along the water and sylvan paths and feed the ducks in a Monetlike pond.

The landscape architect's great love is trees, which Vancouver requites with four hundred thousand specimens, at their most abundant in this end of the city. A third of them line the public streets and boulevards, eighty thousand are shade trees, and sixty thousand flowering (the city may have more cherry and plum trees that blossom than does Tokyo, which commemorates their arrival each spring). "Trees evoke memories, create longing and orient us in space," Cornelia Oberlander says. "They tell the seasons and anticipate change. Without trees, our immediate landscape has no sense of place, no scale, no context."

She praises the legacy of Frederick Todd, a tree-loving Montreal landscape architect hired by the Canadian Pacific Railway around 1910 to help lay out the elite, once-discriminatory subdivision of Shaughnessy. This area between Oak and Arbutus, West 16th and 41st, remains an enclave of wide, shaded boulevards and mansions on lots as large as half a hectare, but the president of a Japanese multinational now might live next door to a German baron. And many of its grand residences have become boarding houses, some even community homes for the physically and mentally handicapped.

The moneyed moved on to Southwest Marine Drive, where three-hectare properties command jaw-dropping views of the Fraser River and Vancouver Island. One is the French Regency Malkin estate (built in 1925 by a pioneer millionaire of the food-distributing Malkin family); another, the Spanish Colonial Revival *Casa Mia* (built six years later by a scion of the brewing and distilling Reifel family).

KIKU HAWKES

Somewhere between these two areas geographically, if downscale from both, sit a couple of relentlessly middle-class neighbourhoods. Oakridge, with its melange of Jewish and Asian families, prefers to conduct its commercial congress at the first shopping centre to open within the city itself (in 1959); Kerrisdale allows its residents a discreet low-rise business district along 41st Avenue (*where mothers in velvet jogging suits push prams*, as poet George Bowering put it).

Westward lie the heights of Arbutus, Mackenzie, and Dunbar, elevated in altitude yet another step down the socio-economic scale (it was in a Dunbar home where Greenpeace was conceived). To the north, overlooking the False Creek waterfront, sprout the condos and apartment towers of the Fairview Slopes. Towards UBC are the tonier homes of Point Grey, which rise in price as they descend to sea level; those on the water constitute a Millionaires' Row. Kits Point has much the same harbour view, but cheaper housing stock. It's the showpiece of once-funky Kitsilano, where hippies frolicked along Fourth Avenue in the '60s, to be replaced by yuppies three decades on.

The West Side embraces other areas, as diverse as Cambie in the east — which seems as self-effacing as Vancouver's hard-edged City Hall, which has its home here — and the southernmost districts of multiple-dwelling Marpole and single-housing Southlands, where residents play golf and ride horses on the Fraser flats.

If Cornelia Oberlander were to choose her most special place on this side of Vancouver, she would look no farther than her own backyard. She has gardens of moss and vegetables and a mini-orchard with apple trees planted for each of her three children. From her kitchen window, she can see West Vancouver's Lighthouse Park and the Coast Mountains she now loves, the seascape of the Strait of Georgia in the distance, and the forest of Pacific Spirit Park immediately below. "The majestic trees greet me every morning," she says, "and tell me of the eternity of nature."

False Creek 1958

FRED HERZOG

West Siders and others gather at the food-and-fun village of Granville Island, the saucer-shaped Planetarium, the Folk Music Festival at Jericho Beach Park, and the cliffside campus of the University of British Columbia.

The West Side is an urban oasis of greenery and natural grace

AL HARVEY

GORDON J. FISHER/IMAGE FINDERS

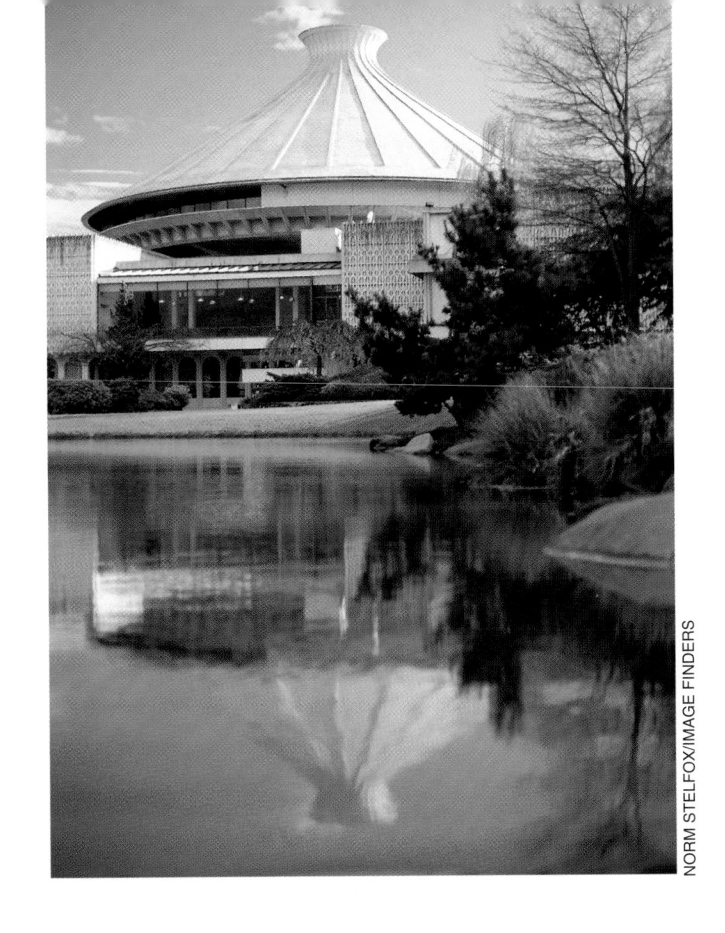

NORM STELFOX/IMAGE FINDERS

AL HARVEY

GORDON J. FISHER/IMAGE FINDERS

ANNIE GRIFFITHS BELT/IMAGE FINDERS

KEN STRAITON/IMAGE FINDERS

THOMAS BRUCKBAUER/IMAGE FINDERS

From seaside Kitsilano Beach to hilltop Queen Elizabeth Park, the West Side is sylvan avenues of flowering trees and some of the city's better homes and gardens.

Window Display

1958

FRED HERZOG

AL HARVEY

Busy beaches and sylvan streetscapes define this side of the city

AL HARVEY

AL HARVEY

KOOS DYKSTRA/IMAGE FINDERS

AL HARVEY

Chinese elders practise tai chi by the Bloedel Conservatory as children frolic in the fields and streets of neighbourhoods nicely distanced from the ferment of downtown.

AL HARVEY

'Round-every-corner parks merge with eminently livable neighbourhoods

BERNIE PAWLIK

AL HARVEY

Home Free

Dan Nomura remembers camping overnight as a kid on Shady Island, a skinny strip of escapism lying just off the waterfront in Steveston. He would fish the Fraser River for Dolly Vardens and oolichans and sell them for a dollar a bucket. Angle for sticklebacks amid the bulrushes in the neighbourhood ditches. Race through the open fields after long-legged cranes, trying to catch those Japanese symbols of good luck. Most of all, he recalls the sense of community he felt living among two thousand Japanese-Canadian fishermen and their families in this maritime village near urban Vancouver. During the Second World War they had endured dislocation and internment camps and the forced sale of almost everything they owned — and had come back home to raise their families and start all over again, finally freed from the prejudice constraining them since the turn of the century.

Today Steveston has been swallowed up in the neighbouring city of Richmond, at the mouth of the Fraser on the southern flanks of Vancouver, and its foreshore has been appealingly revitalized as a tourist attraction. Housing subdivisions, seafood restaurants, and gift shops have risen where canneries once stood. While some fishermen still sell their catch on the docks, the federal government has curtailed the West Coast fishing season, and the Japanese-Canadian community has dispersed as their children move into steadier occupations.

Dan Nomura is one of the minority who remained in the industry. He is a vice-president of the Canadian Fishing Company of Vancouver, whose century-old Steveston plant is being restored as a Canadian heritage site, a memorial to the Japanese, Chinese, native Indians, and other Canadians who processed salmon and herring at the Gulf of Georgia Cannery. Living in Richmond — only a few blocks from the mudflats where he grew up in a long row of $30-a-month cannery houses — the forty-year-old Nomura treasures the few remaining signs of Steveston's Japanese past. The Buddhist church, where he attends funerals of family friends. And the gracefully designed complex that houses the Steveston Martial Arts Centre, a seniors' drop-in centre, and a Japanese-language school where he sends his children twice a week. Yet it's not the same as it once was. "The Japanese influence is being lost," he says.

Dan Nomura as a child of Japanese-Canadian parents in 1964, and as a vice-president of the Canadian Fishing Company today.

There is irony in his regret. For while Japanese-Canadians no longer live in recognizable clusters of cannery houses, and there are few Chinese-Canadians processing fish, Steveston and its parent, Richmond, now have Canada's highest concentration of residents with an Asian heritage — about thirty per cent of the city's 130,000 people, the majority of Chinese descent. Investors from Hong Kong, Taiwan, and Japan are spending hundreds of millions of dollars here to create the largest conglomeration of Asian shopping malls outside Asia. Among developers of major department stores, hotels, and office complexes are such influential names as the Kuok family of Hong Kong and Malaysia, and Mitsui, the Japanese trading empire. About seventy per cent of all land in Richmond's downtown core is Asian-owned; half the money in new housing is Asian. Little wonder the local Chamber of Commerce publishes its information brochure in Cantonese and sponsors dinners for immigrants from Hong Kong, Singapore, the Philippines, and Korea.

All this fresh capital complements the continuing investments that have made Richmond a centre for high-technology, automotive and furnishing firms — and the manufacturing and distribution hub of Western Canada. The city owes some of its success to the Vancouver International Airport that lies within its boundaries. Asia's premier gateway to North America, Vancouver International handles more sea-air cargo than any competitor on the west coast of the continent. Already Canada's second-busiest airport, it was recently privatized amid plans to spend $750 million in expanding and improving facilities.

The airport has absorbed most of Sea Island, one of twenty-five islands that form Richmond. The largest is Lulu, christened by a pioneering colonel in Britain's Corps of Royal Engineers for a young San Francisco actress who entertained the colonists.

Richmond itself, incorporated in 1879, was named for an immigrant family's home town in Australia. Three-quarters of its flatlands rise no more than two metres above sea level. From the start, in the 1860s, settlers had to hand-build dykes and drainage systems to ward off river and sea. They had immensely rich soil to farm. Richmond eventually became the blueberry capital of B.C. and the cranberry capital of North America, and during the 1950s one of its many dairy farms had the largest herd of Holstein cattle in Canada.

Now houses have replaced the farms; Dan Nomura points out a subdivision in Steveston that he knew as expansive fields of Chinese cabbage. His grandparents came to Canada in the 1920s, more than two decades after the first Japanese emigrated here. His father, Junichi, was born in Steveston but schooled in Japan. Returning at sixteen, he fished with his older brother along the Fraser — Japanese-Canadians weren't allowed to harvest the open sea — and out of the half-dollar they got for every sockeye caught, they paid five cents for lodging in a cannery house. Somehow, Junichi Nomura managed to buy his own nine-metre wooden gillnetter. That was 1941. On December 7, Japan bombed Pearl Harbor.

The federal government forced him, like every other Japanese-Canadian fisherman, to sell his boat. The cannery gave him $400, less than half what it was worth. "We were angry for awhile," he says now. "But you can't do anything." Ordered to move from the coast, he wound up on a sugar-beet farm and in a winter logging camp in Alberta. He was among those Joy Kogawa described in her novel *Obasan* as "the fishermen who are flung from the sea to flounder in the dust of the prairies." In 1949 he came back to Steveston. "I feel more home here," Junichi says. On money borrowed from a cannery, he bought another gillnetter and managed to pay off the $2,400 in one year, fishing anywhere he wanted with a unrestricted licence. A year later, he was introduced to a young Japanese-Canadian seamstress named Sakie. After what he calls an arranged marriage — "About time to marry," a friend of her father told him — they started a family of four.

Growing up, Dan doesn't remember feeling any prejudice from the white community. "Maybe I never felt discriminated against because my parents never openly discussed how they were treated during the war — until ten years ago." A deckhand for Junichi, he admired his father's independence and courage. After earning a zoology

GRAHAM OSBORNE

degree from the University of British Columbia and working as a fish biologist, Dan went back for his master's degree. And, in an elegant blending of generations, Dan called upon his father's practical experience to help write his innovative MA thesis about how electrolysis — exchange of ions — creates metal corrosion in fishboats that can repel salmon. Two B.C. companies later developed equipment to control the amount of voltage generated by boats.

Work as a quality-control manager for a fishermen's cooperative led him to a job as supervisor of technical services for the Canadian Fishing Company, where as a vice-president he's now responsible for U.S. operations in San Francisco and Alaska, as well as sales of herring roe and frozen salmon to the Japanese market. The first time he went to Japan, he stepped out into the airport and, much taller than the locals, stared out over a sea of black heads. That wasn't the only way he felt different. "I thought I was going to find my homeland," he recalls. "But I soon figured out that Japan wasn't where I belonged, that Canada wasn't a temporary place."

Although he's married to an Irish-Canadian and realizes his real roots are in this country, he hasn't forgotten his heritage. He serves on the board of the Japanese-language school their children attend in Steveston — where, given the sumptuous ethnic mix of the community, they should grow up as comfortably Asian-Canadian as their father did.

1958

FRED HERZOG

Steveston's Town Centre

Steveston's foreshore has become a place for pleasure seekers, promenading tourists, and Sunday anglers – as well as commercial fishermen, whose boats are seen at right with Washington's Mount Baker as a backdrop.

Richmond's twenty-five islands are ringed by river and sea

FRED HERZOG

FRED HERZOG

ALBERT CHIN/IMAGE FINDERS

PETER TIMMERMANS

Vancouver International Airport is Asia's premier gateway to North America

Now more noted for transportation and high tech, Richmond has a pastoral past that survives in farms like this one, *below*, growing cranberries.

Vancouver Airport

1958

FRED HERZOG

KAJ SVENSSON

GRAHAM OSBORNE

FRED HERZOG

FRED HERZOG

Steveston has a slower, quieter pace, where only the gentle sounds of honking snow geese and chugging fishboats disturb the peace.

PETER TIMMERMANS

Today, even more than in the past, the rich Asian culture flavours Richmond

AL HARVEY

KARL SPREITZ

AL HARVEY

Buddhist and Sikh temples flourish in a city where thirty percent of the population, and half the money spent on new housing, is Asian.

PETER TIMMERMANS

The Urban Peasant

He was in his forties, a partner in an engineering firm, when complications from a leg infection put him in hospital. He was locked in a body cast for almost a year. That's when, to stay sane, he decided to write. His marriage broke up soon afterwards and, living on his own, a neophyte writer and a virtual pauper, he would scrounge the remains of vegetables being cleaned at the back of supermarkets. That's when, to survive, James Barber first became an urban peasant.

PACIFIC PRESS

Flash forward more than two decades. Now he can be seen daily on television across the continent, in Canada on the CBC and in the United States on The Learning Channel, preaching his own philosophy of fast food — savoury dishes, prepared simply, quickly, and inexpensively. The series is called *The Urban Peasant,* the same name gracing one of his seven cookbooks, which he describes as "a book mostly of pleasure, a collection of things I've eaten, cooked and enjoyed in half the countries of the world. Most of it is simple, peasant food, using ingredients which are available at most supermarkets."

Perhaps no one epitomizes the alternative lifestyle of Vancouver more than this pewter-bearded, moon-faced man with a monklike tonsure and a distinctly unmonastic approach to living. His is an offbeat city of food and festivals, of East Side markets and East Hastings steambaths, of cultural options and ethnic diversity. Approaching his seventh decade, with the energy and enthusiasms of someone half his age, he continues to write the city's most passionate prose about wining, dining, and related indulgences, in a city that goes ga-ga over food. His column appears in *The Georgia Straight,* the weekly tabloid that in its choice of topics still carries echoes of its counter-culture past, despite moving downtown from Kitsilano's Fourth Avenue, the main drag of what was once Vancouver's hippie scene.

James Barber is downtown now too, in Gastown, where down-and-outers share the sidewalks with summertime tourists and year-round artist and yuppie residents slowly infiltrating Vancouver's oldest streets. He owns a two-level condo in Mission House, which used to be the Anglican Church's turn-of-the-century distribution point for overseas brides lured here to marry local men. Next door is The Four Sisters Co-op, an internationally acclaimed social-housing complex, and across the street a railyard fronting on the working harbour. Despite his address, he is living much less like a hippie these days: the condos in his gentrified building list for a few hundred thousand dollars and his capacious wooden deck has a cityscape and seaward view to the sails of Canada Place.

The story starts during the Second World War. The British-bred Barber was a young special-duty soldier, sneaking into occupied France to set up shortwave links with the Resistance. It was there — in his own mess kit and in French farmwives' kitchens — that he discovered the basics of cooking. He later refined his techniques under the tutelage of an older Belgian fan dancer with whom he lived in Brussels. After marrying an Englishwoman, moving to Canada and winding up in hospital, he talked his way into a job as freelance theatre and ballet critic for the Vancouver *Province* and eventually persuaded the paper to buy his restaurant-and-food column. A few years ago he was even co-owner of an Italian restaurant along the East Side's spirited Commercial Drive — Little Italy — near his own home at the time, as well as home to an immigrant service organization called MOSAIC, of which he was a long-time president.

All of these strands — cooking, culture, and cosmopolitan influences — come together in James Barber's epicurean way of life. Listen to the man talk about his Vancouver: "If you react to the city, it becomes an urban dance. You can wander the back lanes of Chinatown and hear the clickety-clickety-click clatter of mah-jong tiles. Or go down to the steam baths on East Hastings and see whole Finnish families having a good time for twelve bucks. On Commercial Drive when I ask a butcher, 'What do you do with that?,' Italian women standing around will chip in and finally four of us will be discussing what to do with a piece of meat. Then I'll leave and hear the pitter-patter of feet and a woman will come up to me and say: 'You don't take notice of them; *I* show you.'... In winter, you can buy baby artichokes there and bite the ends off — with the Italians there's no foreplay....The Drive is extremely polyglot: Latin Americans, Koreans, Vietnamese. It's getting a bit flaky now, but it's still alive and vital with a big art scene."

A frequent pleasure is Granville Island, on False Creek below the Granville Street Bridge. It has one of the great public markets of North America, 3,753 square metres of fresh seafood and meats, fruits and vegetables, bakery and specialty goods, wine and flowers, cappuccino bars and crafts stalls. James Barber likens the Saturday-morning socializing at the market to the Spanish form of courtship, the ritualistic *paseo*, a circular evening promenade in a city square. "Food is tangible," he says. "It's culture made manifest."

The island used to be 14.5 hectares devoted exclusively to industry. In the late '70s, an unusually enlightened federal government helped transform it into a pay-its-own-way village of potters and printmakers, woodworkers and glass-blowers, architects and lawyers. In place of nail factories and warehouses, although sometimes within the shells of the same historic tin-sheathed structures, stand the Emily Carr College of Art and Design and a children's arts school, playgrounds and a community centre, houseboats and a hotel, three theatres and a rehearsal and performance space, several restaurants, gift shops and a kids' store, a boatworks and a cottage brewery — and the lone remaining heavy industry, Ocean Cement.

The island plays host to the annual Festival of Fools, the Comedy Festival, and the Vancouver International Writers Festival. The city's social scene brims with such festive events, most of them celebrating less-mainstream pursuits than the Children's Festival (the world's first) and the Sea Festival (featuring the eccentric Nanaimo-Vancouver Bathtub Race). Spring brings festivals devoted to wine, kites, and dragon boats; in summer, jazz, salmon, folk music, fireworks, early music and chamber music; and in the fall, international film and fringe theatre.

Theatrical innovation is well-served throughout the year at the Vancouver East Cultural Centre — The Cultch — a former church, nine decades old, that remains one of Canada's best multipurpose performance spaces. It's one of two East End institutions that celebrate the culturally novel. The other is the Western Front, a combination co-op and salon of avant-garde artists that over the past twenty years conjured up such characters as Dr. Brute (Eric Metcalfe, who painted leopard spots on anything that stood still) and Mr. Peanut (Vincent Trasov, whose top-hatted, monocled alter ego drew a large vote running for Vancouver's mayoralty). The Front survives into the '90s as a home for performance artists who invite the public to their antic happenings. As James Barber remarks, "Vancouver is doubly blessed — not just that it's beautiful, but like the west side of most countries, it's more creative, looser."

Loose enough to allow him to keep pursuing his urban peasanthood, as he still does from time to time, in what he euphemistically calls "back-lane harvesting." Baldly put, this means either helping oneself to food that grows wild in the city or swiping it from branches that hang over back fences. "I have very strict rules," he insists. "You never take more than one of anything. Never take anything if there are less than six. I know where in the city to get hazelnuts, black walnuts, and good edible chestnuts, and one of the best places to find mushrooms — Mountain View Cemetery at Fraser and 33rd, where all the Ukrainian ladies go to pick them. And you can wander up and down the lanes in the East End, all those Italian gardens where they're growing...." His eyes afire, his lips alive in a smile, James Barber rolls on with the passion of a peasant at harvest time.

GRAHAM OSBORNE

James Barber, as TV chef, food columnist, and author today, and as newspaper critic in 1971.

MARJA BERGEN

R. HAMAGUCHI/IMAGE FINDERS

FRED HERZOG

Vancouver alternatives: greenswards to unwind everywhere, even downtown, *top*; festivals of Dragon Boats and Fools fill the calendar; Bard on the Beach brings Shakespeare to the shore; and Granville Island, *opposite,* offers a cornucopia of cultural pursuits from theatres to art galleries.

AL HARVEY

PETER TIMMERMANS

Granville Island has, among much else, one of the great public markets of North America

PETER TIMMERMANS

FUKUHARA/IMAGE FINDERS

Fuelling Vancouverites are a passion for food and for fun set outdoors in their spectacular environment: alfresco dining, Far Eastern cuisine and West Coast seafood, kite-flying in Vanier Park, the Karen Jamieson dancers at the Plaza of Nations, and pet portraits in Stanley Park.

AL HARVEY

AL HARVEY

Cooking, culture, and cosmopolitan influences come together in an epicurean way of life

AL HARVEY

AL HARVEY

FRED HERZOG

1956

Paris Cafe

BERNIE PAWLIK

PETER TIMMERMANS

Food, culture, and escapism are where you find them in alternative Vancouver: mushrooms in Mountain View Cemetery; innovative theatre in the Vancouver East Cultural Centre and performance art at the Western Front; and uncommon quiet on a beach in lively Kitsilano, once home to the city's counter-culture.

MICHAEL MORRIS

FRED HERZOG/IMAGE FINDERS

A true urban peasant finds pleasure in the liveliest – and sometimes the unlikeliest – places

Suburban Pleasures

It is the very model of a modern major suburbia. Burnaby became British Columbia's third-largest city in its centenary year of 1992; before then, the district municipality of 150,000 residents had the ambiguous distinction of being considered a suburban extension of Vancouver. This was a community that, until the vast Metrotown commercial core developed during the last decade, had no recognizable centre, no beating urban heart. As a home-town journalist once wrote, "To grow up in Burnaby is to grow up in a state of mind rather than an actual entity... it's neither here nor there. It is a place that people pass through on their way to and from Vancouver."

Or live in. With its hundred-plus parks, its easy acceptance of ethnic variety, its respected educational centres serving the province's Lower Mainland — and its sanctuarylike separateness from the temptations of the Big Town looming on its western boundary — Burnaby has always seemed an exemplary place in which to raise a family. If this city attracts any attention beyond its borders, it seems to do so with an uncommon sense of decency. Burnaby's contenders for *The Guinness Book of World Records* over the years are a case in point: the world's largest junior hockey tournament (ninety-eight teams during one Christmas event) and the world's largest crock of gruel, concocted by high-school students to promote their production of *Oliver!* One of the darlings of Hollywood — the boyish Michael J. Fox, who so personified American small-town values in the *Back to the Future* film series — was raised in this epitome of the serene Canadian suburb, paying his dues as a drama student performing children's fables in local elementary schools.

The Kimura Parker family at a graduation recital in 1977, and today, *opposite*, in Burnaby's Playground of the Gods.

And two of Canada's finest concert pianists, along with their musically talented sister, grew up here. They were members of an extended family of Japanese and English stock that both drew on and contributed to the qualities that have given Burnaby its purposeful reputation. Elizabeth, a pianist and singer, and Jamie and Jon Kimura Parker are among the city's most artistically gifted products. Jon — Jackie to his friends — won Britain's Leeds International Piano Competition in 1984; *The Washington Post* says the thirty-four-year-old has "a kind of magic and poetry others of his generation can't discover." Jamie, four years his junior and much less flamboyant, has had a national reputation since winning the Canada Council award as the country's most talented young classical performer in 1988. Three years earlier, their kid sister, a decade younger than Jackie, earned a Canadian gold medal for performance in her final Royal Conservatory of Music piano exam. With her degree from the University of British Columbia, where she also studied voice, she's considering a career in music therapy.

Their parents' story is as extraordinary. In 1950, as John Parker was about to enter UBC to study pharmacy, he began corresponding with a pen pal in Japan, a high-school student named Keiko Kimura. Their relationship, born of common intellectual interests, blossomed over six years to the point where, sight unseen, John sent her an engagement ring. The following year, she graduated among the top students in English literature at Tokyo Women's Christian University and emigrated to Canada; twenty days later, she married John Parker and settled with the young pharmacist in Burnaby. (Much later, she became a member of The Jane Austen Society, presenting papers on the English novelist to international conferences and translating her works into Japanese.)

Mrs. Parker continued earlier piano studies with her brother-in-law, Edward Parker, an accomplished teacher who has tutored hundreds of local pianists in the decades since. She started teaching piano, too, and instructing in music theory. Together they have had a profound influence on the musical life of Burnaby — including the careers of the Kimura Parker children. While their classics-loving father taught them to read before first grade, their mother and their uncle persevered with them at the piano. Jackie first performed publicly at the age of five with the Vancouver Youth Orchestra — he was so small he got lost in the violin section and had to be led by the conductor to the piano.

The family shared more than music. They had a Sunday tradition of picking up hamburgers at the local White Spot and coming home to watch *Star Trek*; parents and kids alike can still flash the cleft-handed Vulcan salute.

Their home in Willingdon Heights backs on to Beeches Park, where Liz recalls picking salmonberries, hunting crayfish in the stream, and climbing among the dense mini-forest. "This is a nice, clean, happy suburb," she says. Older brother Jackie, who now lives in Manhattan, has some of the same pleasant recollections as well as the bittersweet memory of practising to the sound of kids cheering each other at a Little League game across the lane. Among the three of them, the Kimura Parkers won hundreds of piano competitions. The earliest were at festivals sponsored by the Burnaby Clef Society, a grassroots community organization that continues to award scholarships and arrange recitals for student musicians. "It's good for a kid to be constantly reinforced with the idea that music is a joyful thing," Jackie Parker says in praise of the society.

They attended Alpha Secondary, where quiet Jamie was elected president without running for the position. The student body was heavily Italian- and Chinese-Canadian; "being half-Japanese," Jackie jokes, "I always felt ethnically perfect." The school reflected the multicultural mix of Burnaby, where a Danish bakery might rub shoulders with a West Indian spice shop and an East Indian grocery.

There had been Sikh and Chinese labourers in the logging mills that were springing up during the birth of the municipality (which was named for Robert Burnaby, who became a member of the B.C. legislature after serving as a key aide to the contingent of Royal Engineers laying out the Lower Mainland). Industry — which now includes specialty manufacturing, wholesale distribution, communications, and high technology — has never imposed itself too weightily on Burnaby. The city prospers because of its location at the geographical hub of Greater Vancouver and the centre of major highway and transit systems. It has always been strategically positioned: Canada's first electric interurban tramline ran from Vancouver to New Westminster through Burnaby on the same route now being used for the rapid-transit SkyTrain.

Burnaby's handy access and attractive character have been luring suburbanites since at least 1912, when realtors were boasting of "the equable climate, the scenic beauty, and the proximity of Vancouver, which make this an ideal place for permanent residence." That's still true, although certain other things have changed. Until the 1950s it was the province's only electoral district without a liquor store. It did, however, have Canada's first drive-in theatre. Now the city has no drive-in but six liquor stores. And spreading atop 365-metre-high Burnaby Mountain is Simon Fraser University, with a sleek concrete design by Arthur Erickson and Geoffrey Massey that proved futuristic enough to serve as a setting for science-fiction movies. The instant campus, built in only seventeen months, opened in 1965 — a year after the esteemed B.C. Institute of Technology. Beside BCIT stand the Open Learning Agency and the Discovery Parks complex of high-tech companies.

GRAHAM OSBORNE

The beauty that brought the first residents to Burnaby still abounds. Ten per cent of all the vegetables produced in the Lower Mainland are grown here, in gardens that have long been tilled by Chinese in broad-rimmed sun hats. And then there are the urban parks — oh, the parks! More than a fifth of the city is green space. Central Park, created a year before the municipality's birth, is ninety hectares of Douglas fir and jogging and cycling trails, a pitch-and-putt, and a swimming pool. Deer Lake, which native legend says is linked to Vancouver's False Creek by subterranean tunnel, offers fishing and boating. Burnaby Lake has an interpretive nature house to enhance a wildlife sanctuary harbouring great blue herons and other untamed fowl. Not surprisingly, the Wildlife Rescue Association of B.C. makes its home in this city, where on Burnaby Mountain the mule deer and the coyotes still play.

The mountaintop is also the *Playground of the Gods* — which is the title of an astonishing piece of art, a forest of poles carved like totems by an eminent Japanese sculptor. The work commemorates a quarter-century of friendship between Burnaby and its sister city of Kushiro, Japan. Two of its figures, a killer whale and a bird, point symbolically west, across the Pacific, where a young Canadian man once sent an engagement ring to a Japanese woman and founded a musical family.

Braids of green embroider this park-rich model suburb

PETER TIMMERMANS

PETER TIMMERMANS

Industry seldom imposes itself too weightily on Burnaby, which is more noted for its multicultural mix and a hundred-plus parks.

WES BERGEN/DIARAMA

AL HARVEY

The shopping magnet of Metrotown seems an anomaly in a city whose classic scenes include the Burnaby Art Gallery in summer, the Deerholme heritage house in winter, and produce farms in autumn.

FRED HERZOG

FRED CHAPMAN/DIARAMA

Sleek skyscrapers are only starting to punctuate the gardenlike setting

AL HARVEY

FRED CHAPMAN/DIARAMA

Elements of the Burnaby lifestyle: living above the clouds on Capitol Hill, sailing on Deer Lake, and learning on the lawn of the futuristic-looking Simon Fraser University.

FRED CHAPMAN/DIARAMA

GRANT V. FAINT

Higher education reaches a peak atop Burnaby Mountain

AL HARVEY

FRED CHAPMAN/DIARAMA

The Image

Christmas on Division Street, a charming TV movie that has become an instant seasonal classic, was filming on some of the meanest streets of Vancouver during the summer of 1991. Veteran actor Hume Cronyn and *The Wonder Years'* young Fred Savage were doing a scene in a back lane on the Downtown East Side, behind what might be the grungiest single block in the city. And while the cameras rolled, drug addicts were shooting up just along the alley. Nearby, on the final day of filming, young punks kicked and stabbed an old man in front of a horrified movie crew.

This off-screen action is far from the image that Vancouver likes to present in billing itself as Canada's Film City. By 1990 Greater Vancouver was ranked third-busiest among movie-production capitals in North America, and within two years film companies were spending more than $211 million annually here; in '92 they produced eleven television series, thirty-four TV movies, and sixteen feature films. The city has the reputation of being a director's dream in which to film, with local crews that are more cooperative (and cheaper), and citizens less jaded about movie-making than in either Los Angeles or New York. And with a versatile metropolitan environment and a dazzling natural backdrop, that can turn Vancouver into one big movie set.

With some caveats. That sea-and-mountain setting, and the very fact that the city isn't an urban jungle, can be a drawback to film companies, as local producer Colleen Nystedt points out: "This is a small city with a certain amount of variety, but we have no true slums. As a production manager I've doubled Vancouver as Boston (for *The Accused,* with Jodie Foster), Philadelphia (*Christmas on Division Street),* East Germany (a *McGyver* TV episode), and anywhere in the Pacific Northwest. But I can't do brownstones or row housing here, and you have to be careful to avoid the mountains — you're always shooting south, away from them."

Not always. In '93, as co-executive producer, she was up in the North Shore mountains to shoot *City Boy,* financed by the U.S. Public Broadcasting System, the Canadian Broadcasting Corporation, and the British Columbia Film Commission — the first international co-production initiated from B.C. "Physically," she says, "that was a hard picture, shlepping all that heavy equipment up and down the mountains in the rain."

In her mid-thirties, with a dynamism that overflows her five-foot-two frame, Colleen Nystedt runs her own embryonic film company, New City Productions. Its name not only derives from her ex-husband's Germanic surname, but also from her vision of Vancouver's promise as a young and vigorous movie centre. "I know my way around this town," she says. "In school the city was my classroom. I've watched it grow and change as a member of a family that was part of the evolution."

Her father is Walter Hardwick, who taught urban geography at the University of British Columbia, wrote a book about Vancouver, and served as a young-Turk alderman in the 1960s and later as B.C.' s deputy minister of urban affairs. As a teenager, Colleen wrote a detailed history of her Kerrisdale neighbourhood, and, to claim some of her busy Dad's time, would discuss city-council issues with him. She recalls marching through Gastown in her poncho to help save the area from freeway development.

GRAHAM OSBORNE

Colleen Nystedt, as a successful movie producer today, and in 1962 as the child of a prominent urban geographer.

At twenty-five she was a youth delegate with the federal Liberal Party (and more recently, a member-at-large of the B.C. Women's Liberal Commission). By that time she had a UBC degree in geography and political science, a job with the City of Victoria's planning department, an artist/botanist husband, and the first of two children.

They were living in a grand old house her father had bought in the provincial capital when one day in 1983 there was a fateful knock on the door. "It changed my life forever," Colleen Nystedt says. It was a location scout wanting to use their home for a scene in *The Glitter Dome,* a TV cop movie. Enthralled by the impact of film — "People's heroes are in entertainment and I could do more to shape public opinion through the mass media than I could through politics" — she set out to learn everything she could about the business. She learned so well, so quickly, that the following year she became office coordinator and then assistant location manager for the production company filming Michael Cimino's *Year of the Dragon,* set in New York but shot partly in Victoria and Vancouver.

After stints as a location manager for several made-in-Vancouver TV movies, a Disney Channel series, and her first major feature, *The Accused,* she graduated to production manager — among her credits are Sandy Wilson's *American Boyfriend* and *Crooked Hearts,* again with Jodie Foster. For that one, her brother Doug was construction manager and brother Gord location manager, as they were for *Christmas on Division Street.*

After completing *City Boy,* an environmental parable set at the turn of the century, her hope was to fulfill a six-picture deal for family TV movies with Bonneville Producers Group of L.A. "I can film Vancouver as average Middle America, average urban centre," she says, "but what I'd like to be able to do is shoot more of the Marine Building, more of the cruise-ship terminal — I want to make Vancouver *Vancouver.*"

However it's disguised, the city is bound to be showing up more and more often on screen. A film complex in Burnaby houses four studios, including the continent's largest special-effects stage. North Vancouver has the country's largest full-service studio, where Stephen Cannell produces more than $800 million worth of TV series a year, among them *Wiseguy* and *21 Jump Street.* And Vancouver's Kitsilano is the home of Spelling Television Canada, which has produced such small-screen series as *Beverly Hills 90210.* Not long ago, Vancouverites could have bumped into Burt Reynolds and Katharine Hepburn filming *The Man Upstairs,* Charles Bronson and Christopher Reeve *(Seawolf),* Robert De Niro and Ellen Barkin *(This Boy's Life),* and Patty Duke and Loretta Swit *(Friends to the End).*

Greater Vancouver teems with settings and attractions that may be visual clichés to locals, but could well be fresh images to the world's movie-goers: for example, North Vancouver's Capilano Suspension Bridge, Vancouver's cruise-ship terminal, the Royal Hudson steam train, and the aquarium and totem poles of Stanley Park. With the power of contemporary icons, these images adorn tens of thousands of postcards and appear with montonous regularity in the viewfinders of tourists' cameras. And it is just such photographic stereotypes that have helped make tourism Vancouver's number-one industry.

Colleen Nystedt would like to capture some of the familiar images on film. She dreams of doing one chase scene up the fire escape of the old Sun Tower downtown, another on the tram that soars up Grouse Mountain. "I'm part of this place," she says, explaining why she stays in Vancouver to make her movies. "I can't imagine being anywhere else."

KEN STRAITON/IMAGE FINDERS

GORDON J. FISHER/IMAGE FINDERS

A city's icons: an artistic glimpse of the Vancouver Art Gallery; Park Place at tulip time; Canada Place at dawn; and the inevitable Lions Gate Bridge.

KOOS DYKSTRA/IMAGE FINDERS

PETER BENNETT

Fresh eyes, curious minds, bring new beauty to Vancouver's visual clichés

FRED HERZOG

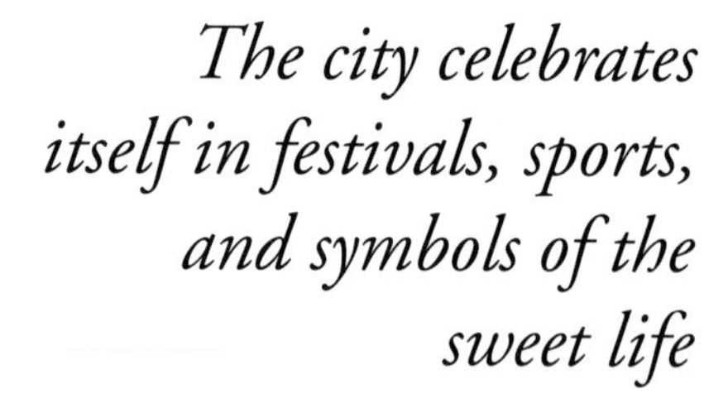

The city celebrates itself in festivals, sports, and symbols of the sweet life

FRED HERZOG

DAVE WATTERS/IMAGE FINDERS

MICHAEL MONG

FRED HERZOG

GUNTER MARX

Old rituals meet modern flash: cricketers in Stanley Park and Japanese-Canadians at an Obon Festival reinforce the city's image as much as fireworks competitions, Indy races, and fast convertibles.

PETER TIMMERMANS

The park of all downtown parks reflects the very best of what we want to be

At dusk, for revelling high-school graduates and meandering couples in love, and at dawn, for joggers rounding the seawall's Brockton Point turn, Stanley Park has moods of gold as well as green.

The C.P.R.'s Princess Patricia

1967

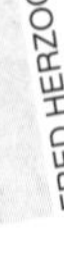

FRED HERZOG

PETER TIMMERMANS

KOOS DYKSTRA/IMAGE FINDERS

Airshow at English Bay

1960

FRED HERZOG

The city as movie set: make-believe against magical sea-and-mountain backdrops

BOB MATHESON

PETER BENNETT

DAVE WATTERS/IMAGE FINDERS

PETER BENNETT

With cityscapes like False Creek and its distinctive Science World dome, and natural settings that are a photographer's dream, little wonder that Vancouver thrives as the continent's third-busiest film-production capital.

AL HARVEY

The Promised City

Eva Lee Kwok is one of the tens of thousands of recent newcomers from across the Pacific who have settled in what commentators are calling North America's first Asian city. But, unlike many of her compatriots, this Malaysian-born Chinese woman came to Vancouver somewhat reluctantly. She had glimpsed the city for the first time in 1967, when she considered it a sleepy, provincial town compared to the London she had just left. Two and a half decades later she continues to observe its imperfections as well as its strengths and promise. "Vancouver must be careful not to be too complacent about its natural beauty and the richness of its immigrant population," she cautions. "We have to grow beyond any smugness, be more open-minded and challenge ourselves. We must contribute our energy and work even harder as a community to develop the city's potential. It's not just the locals — the immigrants themselves become quite smug. And it's easy to do here because we seem to have everything. On the plus side, there are still lots of possibilities for people to take advantage of. Vancouver is like the Canada I came to originally: a land of opportunity."

In fact, Eva Lee, as she was then, came to this country because she wanted to buy a Mustang. Educated as a clinical dietitian in Australia — where she went to escape a suffocatingly formal family life — she earned her master of science at the University of London. Today, the headstrong, independent fifty-year-old insists the impetus that propelled her young self here was the desire to own that sleek Ford sports car. "It was a symbol of speed," she muses, "and you couldn't buy one in England or Europe. And I didn't want to go to the U.S." Instead, she took a job as chief dietitian of a hospital in faraway Trail, deep in the B.C. Interior, and her first major purchase was a blue Mustang.

In 1968, she moved to Saskatoon as an assistant professor in the College of Home Economics at the University of Saskatchewan. For the next twenty years she remained happily in the province — becoming dean of the college, then in '89 the first president of the Saskatchewan Institute of Applied Science and Technology, and a year later the provincial vice-president of the Asia Pacific Foundation of Canada, an independent, non-profit organization based in Vancouver.

Only after marrying Stanley Kwok did she agree to live in Vancouver, in what so many other immigrants seem to consider a Promised City. Until recently her new husband was deputy chairman of Concord Pacific Developments Ltd., which has launched the most ambitious urban-development project in Canada: the $2.5-billion Pacific Place by 2002 will comprise residential towers, social housing, schools, commercial areas, and forty-two acres of parks. There will be 13,500 people living along downtown False Creek on land once dedicated to Expo 86.

It was the world's fair that catalyzed global focus on a cosmopolitan city which then had more than 100,000 Chinese-Canadians, 40,000 Indo-Canadians, 12,000 Japanese-Canadians, and perhaps 10,000 more from Korea and Vietnam. Among overseas investors with this fresh vision of Vancouver was Li Ka-shing, one of Hong Kong's wealthiest businessmen, who dispatched his son, Victor, to study at the University of British Columbia and help set up Concord Pacific in Vancouver. Eventually they hired the Shanghai-educated, locally based architect/developer Stanley Kwok to spearhead the development. The younger Li and Kwok are representative of the special breed of Asian newcomer that has re-energized Vancouver. Some historians say this may be the first time ever that a high-profile array of immigrants has come to a highly developed country like Canada and instantly settled so high up the social scale.

Which is not to say that every recent Asian arrival in Vancouver is well-born and well-heeled. Three-quarters of the non-Canadian immigrants settling in Vancouver are from Asia and the majority hail from Hong Kong, which faces Communist takeover in 1997 (their numbers in B.C. increased by 500 percent between 1986 and 1990). But many of them, lured here to join established relatives, had only modest incomes. Their children make up the majority of English-as-Second-Language (ESL) students in the city's schools — who collectively form the majority of *all* students in the system.

Eva Lee Kwok makes the point that Chinese from Hong Kong and mainland China are only the newest of the ethnic groups who have re-energized Vancouver: "Immigrants from all parts of the world — Italians, Germans, so many others — have contributed." In recent years Central American refugees have more than doubled the number of Spanish-speaking ESL students and created the paradox of Chilean music rocking the Russian Hall on the Downtown East Side and Salvadorian restaurants thriving in the midst of Commercial Drive's Little Italy. Indo-Canadians have established their own strongholds; the area around East 49th and Main can be a scene out of Bombay, teeming with turbaned men and sari'd women. And some Japanese-Canadians continue to patronize shops on downtown Powell Street, the site of their ancestors' earliest community in Vancouver, the turn-of-the-century Japantown.

The city, like the province and the nation, has not always been a gracious host to minorities. As early as 1885, there was a $50 poll tax (later $500) on Chinese immigrants who had been imported to build the transnational railroad, and a law preventing them from buying Crown lands. In 1914, in the infamous *Komogata Maru* incident, Vancouver refused entry to about 150 Sikhs after they waited aboard ship for more than three months. A 1923 law halted all Asian immigration to B.C. And in 1942, most of the city's nine thousand Japanese-Canadian residents were stripped of their homes and fishboats, interned, and sent away from the coast for so-called wartime security reasons. Not until 1949 were they and First Nations people allowed to vote provincially and federally — two years after the franchise was granted to Chinese- and Indo-Canadians.

Eva Lee Kwok, the Malaysian-born Chinese president of an investment corporation today, and a newcomer to Canada in 1967.

GRAHAM OSBORNE

Four decades on, there are still rumblings from a few non-Asian Canadians about "monster houses" being built by the wealthier newcomers from Hong Kong and about jobs supposedly being stolen by the poorer immigrants. It's unfortunately true that a relative handful of young Hong Kong and Vietnamese Chinese are members of the influential gangs lately terrorizing fellow immigrants (prompting the police department to set up an Asian Crime Squad). Yet the more enlightened majority recognizes that most of these new people are injecting rich seasoning and a welcome meatiness into the multicultural stew that is metropolitan Vancouver.

Not only is the continent's second-largest Chinatown being revitalized, but a satellite version is also swelling in suburban Richmond. Three Hong Kong newspapers have Vancouver operations and a Taiwanese paper its own local printing plant; both *The Richmond Review,* a community weekly, and the *Buy and Sell* want-ad tabloid have launched Chinese-language editions. Vancouver's Cathay International Chinese cable-TV channel has fifteen thousand subscribers. Even the racetrack at Exhibition Park has three full-time wickets for Cantonese- and Mandarin-speaking bettors. More symbolically, British Columbia's current lieutenant-governor is David See-chai Lam. At forty-three, the Hong Kong-born banker relocated in Vancouver as a more humble real-estate agent, became a broker for Asian development here, and retired early to become a philanthropist whose largesse includes a $3-million endowment to the University of British Columbia.

The Kwoks, Stanley and Eva Lee, seem equally determined to give back as much as they have received from their new home. Between them, they serve on at least twenty prominent boards — about ten apiece, including those of national banks, provincial crown agencies, civic bodies, and charitable and educational institutions. Eva Lee Kwok is president of her own company, Amara International Investment Corporation, which liaises between Asian investors and local entrepreneurs.

"Vancouver is like a child in late adolescence, the age when you're going to the prom," she says. "The next few years will be very important. From that point of view, we're living in exciting times. But the city needs the right encouragement — the right people in business, the arts and education, to inject the energy and the enthusiasm. We think we've got it good now, but it could be so much better. We need to dream a little bit more."

AL HARVEY

Hong Kong-financed Pacific Place, the most ambitious urban-development project in Canada, is transforming the Expo 86 lands in downtown Vancouver.

MICHEAL MONG

Scenes from a city in transition: saris at an East Indian market on Main Street; kimonos at a Japanese festival; three generations of Filipino women; and a newcomer borne triumphantly aloft by the local mailman.

FRED HERZOG

Trans-Pacific influences are refashioning the very visage of Vancouver and its suburbs

PETER TIMMERMANS

AL HARVEY

FRED HERZOG

Cellular conversations on the street and young Chinese-Canadians in denim and dark glasses coexist with Chinatown's decades-old buildings, ancient New Year's celebrations, and *below left*, the classic Dr. Sun Yat-Sen Garden.

KEN STRAITON/IMAGE FINDERS

THOMAS BRUCKBAUER

Old allegiances are changing as new generations arrive to redefine Chinatown

GUNTER MARX

New World Confectionary

1962

FRED HERZOG

FRED HERZOG

Yesterday: the New World of the Japanese community along Powell Street in the '50s and '60s

Gastown Barber Shop

1959

FRED HERZOG

KOOS DYKSTRA/IMAGE FINDERS

Today: Chinese schools and reverence for Dr. Sun Yat-Sen in counterpoint to street hogs and back-alley restaurants.

FRED HERZOG

GARY FIEGEHEN

GARY FIEGEHEN

AL HARVEY

The fresh wave from Asia is only the latest in a succession of immigrants re-energizing the city

GUNTER MARX

Among the young, cultures begin crossing early, while their elders preserve some of the past, as these Tyrolean dancers do. Latin American immigrants, *right*, transplant their open-air café society.

AL HARVEY

DAVE WATTERS/IMAGE FINDERS

R. HAMAGUCHI

AL HARVEY

FRED HERZOG

Vibrant street life – on the East Side's Commercial Drive or downtown Powell Street, *left* – is bringing together ethnic groups and generations in a city that has an increasing sense of itself as a player on the world stage.

PHOTO OVERLEAF BY AL HARVEY

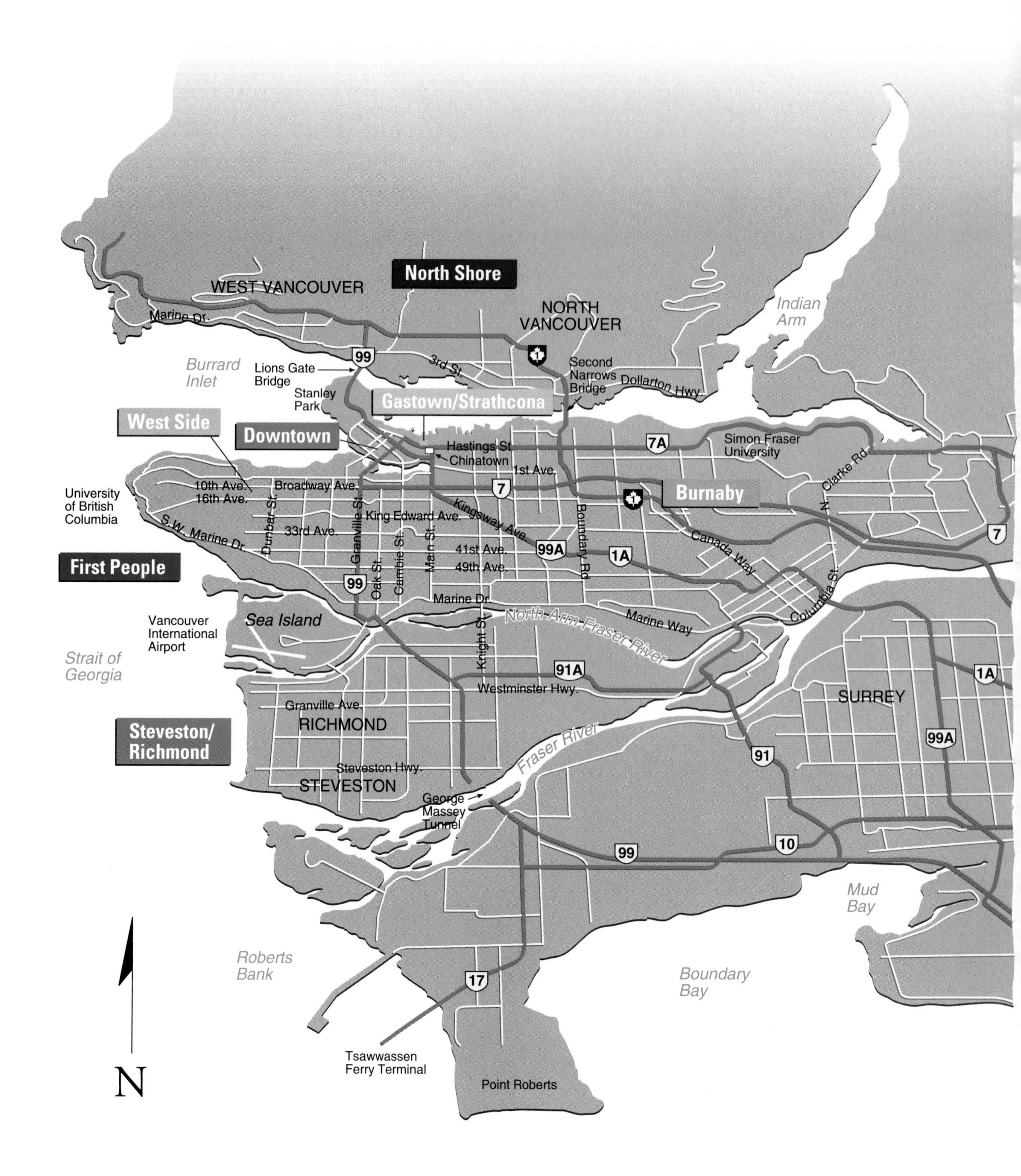
North Shore
WEST VANCOUVER
NORTH VANCOUVER
Indian Arm
Marine Dr.
Burrard Inlet
Lions Gate Bridge
99
3rd St.
Second Narrows Bridge
Dollarton Hwy.
Stanley Park
Gastown/Strathcona
West Side
Downtown
Hastings St.
Chinatown
7A
Simon Fraser University
1st Ave.
N. Clarke Rd.
University of British Columbia
10th Ave.
16th Ave.
Broadway Ave.
7
Burnaby
Dunbar St.
Granville St.
King Edward Ave.
Kingsway Ave.
Boundary Rd.
S.W. Marine Dr.
33rd Ave.
Canada Way
First People
Oak St.
Cambie St.
Main St.
41st Ave.
49th Ave.
99A
1A
Columbia St.
Marine Dr.
Vancouver International Airport
Sea Island
North Arm Fraser River
Marine Way
Strait of Georgia
Knight St.
91A
Westminster Hwy.
SURREY
Granville Ave.
RICHMOND
Steveston/ Richmond
Fraser River
91
Steveston Hwy.
STEVESTON
George Massey Tunnel
99
10
Mud Bay
Roberts Bank
17
Boundary Bay
N
Tsawwassen Ferry Terminal
Point Roberts